THE INNER WORLD

BEYOND THE PRISM OF SENSES:
IN SIMPLE WORDS

MOHAMMAD BABAEE

ISBN: 978-1-4669-6904-9 (sc)
ISBN: 978-1-4669-6905-6 (hc)
ISBN: 978-1-4669-6903-2 (e)

Library of Congress Control Number: 2012921940

Trafford rev. 11/29/2012

 www.trafford.com

North America & international
toll-free: 1 888 232 4444 (USA & Canada)
phone: 250 383 6864 ♦ fax: 812 355 4082

Dedicated to my kindhearted mother

CONTENTS

PREFACE

As far as human beings can remember, the questions "Where do we come from?" and "Where are we going?" have confused us and have not provided any answers. There are enigmas like how the scenario of life ends and who the creator is. What the purpose behind the creation of humankind and the existing universe is, as well as many questions like these, is unanswered. In spite of the long presence human beings have had on earth, no theorist has introduced a convincing answer to these challenging questions yet. Every philosopher has discussed ideas according to the knowledge of their own time. These theories and ideas became invalid or imperfect as knowledge and science advanced through time. Meanwhile, some self-blinded people who were afraid of the unknown for their fanatical beliefs—which is a sign of weakness rather bravery—caused many barbaric wars in order to preserve their beliefs instead of cothinking. Such people are afraid of thinking or envisaging the mysteries of themselves and universe. This just proves their ignorance and unawareness. Conversely, understanding people, who have enough courage and wisdom, have always done their utmost to make people think rather than fight. Likewise, they have obliterated people's panic with their precious guidance. They discovered that the best and safest way is through self-knowledge. However, how and where should it start?

I believe the best and easiest way to gain that knowledge is to study the performance of sense channels completely; these senses function as canals which feed our perception and draw a charming world for us. Because of our incontrovertible and doubtless beliefs in this glamorous world—which are attained through the outlets of our body-caged five senses—we base our ideology on whatever we perceive; and our perception creates our world, thoughts, and reasons. In other words, all beliefs, thoughts, and theories in this material world are based on the knowledge that has been attained from the environment around us via different senses—in a way that beings are not capable of understanding or knowing anything out of our senses' limitations. This implies that human beings can only understand things that they have sensorial-perceptual memory of or perceive via the five senses. When people try to understand what they have heard, they start simulating it with their past memories. They have gained memories via the five senses or have inherited them from their ancestors. It infers that, along with genetic information, parents transfer all their perceptional memories such as tastes, smells, colors, sensations of pain and pleasure, occurrences, sounds, etc., to their baby. However, most of these memories have been stored in our subconscious mind; they remain untouchable for our conscious mind.

Transformation of perceptional memories makes each generation wiser, more intelligent, and more understanding. It is since each child starts accomplishing his awareness from the point that his parents finished. This indicates that at the time of birth, the child's awareness is the same as his parents'. Hence, each child understands things as well as his parents, but he cannot show all his awareness since he is not familiar with common rules such as linguistics, studies, etc. Indeed, with the passing of time, humankind completes its awareness.

Lots of information which human beings receive from their surroundings is not sensorial. These include verbal messages wherein we hear voices and words which cause us to remember things without receiving any signs from our senses. Hence, in order to understand and imagine these messages, a background or earlier memory is necessary. These memories are the foundation of humankind's imagination, thoughts, knowledge, and personality.

People simulate the unknown messages by analyzing their preceding impressions of a similar subject. Afterward, they establish their inner world based on these simulations and form their reasoning, theories, and ideologies based on the world their senses create.

All these memories originated from feelings attained by senses such as tastes, smells, sounds, colors, heat and cold, etc. The most understanding man is the one who has the most active ancestral memories or most personal perceptional memories.

Undoubtedly, there would be many differences between people's viewpoints about whatever they see if the number of people who could not recognize colors was one million times more than the people who could. Namely, those who are color-blind would not understand the reasons of healthy ones for choosing clothes to buy. It is for they cannot distinguish any differences between green and red. To them, the healthy ones have strayed to illusions and superstitions. No one knows what healthy people would look like from their point of view. The color-blind people are not capable of understanding colors because they do not have any impressions of colors in their minds. This means that they are incapable of understanding and visualizing whatever is defined by colors and by color recognition.

That is why people use examples extensively for illustration in education; among them, the most successful teachers are the ones who use a variety of examples so that the audience can choose illustrations that are more relevant to their past perceptional memories in order to imagine or to visualize the subject. However, each audience member's perception would not be the same because of their different understandings of the same subject.

Humankind's knowledge is based on memories experienced via the senses; and the rest is imagination and simulation that they make with their early descriptions, knowledge, and understandings.

Imagine that we just know the color blue and someone tries to teach us colors—other colors. The teacher refers to colors by describing them via making blue more or less strong in our mind. As with the other example, imagine we hear about an unfamiliar taste, smell, etc. We begin to simulate it with our perceptional memories instead of understanding the reality. Therefore, the level of mutual agreement between two beings is associated with how similar their perceptional memories are.

None of us can realize the perceptions of others through talking or studying. People just picture what they see or hear by mixing it with their sensorial memories. This implies that things will be meaningful provided that creatures can draw a picture of them through their memories.

Sensorial Perceptions

Everybody claims that they are right—that they are more intelligent and more logical than others are. According to them, the others are faulty, ignorant, and prejudiced. They are annoyed because people do not understand them; they become irritated when people do not accept their ideas or do not agree with them. Is someone who is defiant—someone whose thoughts are not similar to ours—really guilty and foolish? Have they been involved in the same experiences, feelings, and learning as we have—and still do—during our lifetime? Considering the function and mechanism of our sensorial channels, it is somehow our ignorance and lack of knowledge about our totality and those of others that lead us to prejudge.

If our perception span depends on the range and diversity of our perceptional memory, shall we claim that it is perfect compared to others'? If the answer is negative, then how could we claim that what we name superstition is unreal and what we call reality is true and real? During the daytime, we see many social and personal behaviors of human beings or even animals which seem adorable or blameful from our point of view. Have you ever thought about what you would do if you were in someone else's place with their exact knowledge, experience, feelings, position, and vice versa?

Poetry, art, paintings, and cryptic words of mystics are different tools to express nature, feelings, and perceptions. They make understanding of something easy by using simple examples for the audience. In this manner, they have opened a narrow way to communicate with other people.

Someone who is capable of understanding all perceptional memories of audiences will answer each person differently for the same question. Some responses may seem unreasonable for some people, but actually, each answer would be perfect just for one person at the time. Hence, if someone opposed you or did not understand you, you can be sure that your logic does not conform to his perceptional memories, so you must look for the logic, which is similar to his preceding expressions.

People assume that the boundary between reality and superstition is their senses, naming things outside of their sense territories "superstition" since the only comprehensible language for beings is to perceive objects and things via one of sense channels—through seeing, tasting, smelling, touching, or other feelings. Accordingly, based on this rule, they translate whatever they receive into their understandable language, which is the language of sense (of course, those who memorize the subject instead of understanding it are excluded[1]), and they utilize their sensorial memories that have been gathered throughout the time in this transformation. Therefore, what they build up in their mind is a description of reality rather than reality itself—a description which resulted from summing up previous memories which never became reality.

Some words such as *God, existence, world, afterworld, nonorganics, spirit,* etc., are the words that human beliefs are based on. Therefore, most of the tensions and events that have occurred in the world, society, and even family have been rooted directly or indirectly in people's understanding of these words. Beliefs are mainly comparative, and they are based on one's previous memories since these words cannot be perceived via senses. Hence, the description that people state for themselves or others is the explanation of their

---

[1]   From Sebastian Leitner's point of view, understanding is in company with association of ideas, but memorizing is a companion of recalling the exact word in mind and uttering it, which doesn't lead to conception of the subject.

internal memory rather than reality, or it is only a simulation made by their mind. Therefore, before any judgment in this field, firstly, we must recognize the cage which has surrounded us in this vale and just has limited outlets (with numerous filters) in it. We observe the existing universe through the prism of senses, and we think that we observe reality. We build up all our beliefs based on them and start judging existence, creation, and God while it is essential to have perfect knowledge about these channels and their abilities to find out the validity of received information.

In this book, I have tried to write my ideas—which are the result of many years of working out, troubles, and abstinence—as simply as I could in order to pay my debt to humanity.

BEYOND THE PRISM OF SENSES

Optic Channel

Is what we see a real world?

I hope that you don't get tired by reading the introduction about the five-sense physiology since we need to enter the territory of physiology and physics to achieve conclusion. However, I tried to explain the scientific subjects of the book in such a way that it makes these subjects understandable.

Vision is one of the most important and reliable human senses; it forms 50 percent of our beliefs in a way that people believe in whatever this channel perceives, as well as deny whatever they cannot perceive via this sense. It is good to know that most of the ideas and theories related to the world, afterworld, physics, metaphysics, beings, God, angels, etc., are mainly based on the assumption that visual sense is real and perfect. Therefore, most of theoreticians in physics and metaphysics fields have discussed the world and existing universe from this point of view. Ugly and beautiful, light and darkness, colors, social conventions, shadows, the beauty of a flower or a bird, organic and nonorganic[2] —these originate from this sense. However, do these things show reality? Do we see truly and perfectly? Are the things we see real? In order to get under way to know the totality of ourselves, we must become familiar with the mechanism of our optic channel in order to find a way to discover internal and external secrets. How can we assess the validity of our beliefs or others' thoughts if what we see is not trustable? Review your thoughts and beliefs and then say how much of them are based on the signs which are received via optic channel.

---

[2] All structures that have been built from detectable material and energy are called organic. All structures that do not have any material component, are not detectable or perceptible, and are not known to physics are called nonorganic (e.g., spirit).

THE PHYSIOLOGY OF EYES

Optic Channel

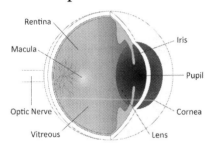

Eyes are the main part of the optic channel. Beings are excited by light; eyes picture the world for our perception and connect us to the external world via a restricted spectrum of waves. The light is projected on the retina after being reflected from nonluminous things or eradiation of luminous things; subsequently, a spectral image of objects and the surroundings is formed.

The retina is made of two layers. The first layer, the slimmer one, is called the pigmented layer. This layer is located between the retina and choroid and contains melanocytes that are in charge of the color black. These pigments cause all lights being absorbed by the eye, and it acts as a darkroom. The second layer, which is thicker as it consists of ten other layers, is called the sensitive retina. In this layer, there are two kinds of light-sensitive cells (photoreceptors) which are known as rods and cones. The diameter of cone and rod cells is about 4.5 microns. Cones that are concentrated in the central part of retina are sensitive to intensive light and provide our eyesight during daylight. These cells are in charge of discerning color. The macula is located in the center of the retina, where most of the cones are. Fovea (yellow stain) is a small concavity in the center of the macula which contains most of the cones. The macula is in charge of central vision and distinguishing colors and details. In dimness, our eyesight is sensitive to blue light rather than red light. Generally, red cones consist of 64 percent of the eye's cone cells; 34 percent of cones are green and only 2 percent of them are blue, but blue cones are more sensitive than the other ones. In most parts of the eye, red, green, and blue cones have formed a cluster shape adjacent to each other. However, in the fovea, the number of blue cones is reduced remarkably. There are approximately six millions cones in our retina. Around the central part of retina, there are about 125 million cells, which are called rods. Sensitivity of these cells to the low light makes our vision possible during the nighttime.

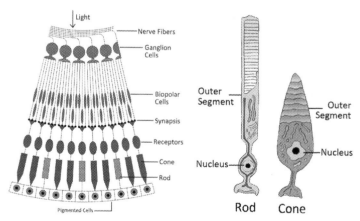

The high density of rods around the retina makes peripheral regions more sensitive, with due attention to the slight light variations in the night. Hence, in order to distinguish peripheral movements better, you must indirectly look to the intended place. This is a way that soldiers can identify enemies in the night. Since, in these conditions, an image will be formed around the retina where rod cells are gathered, it increases the power of eyesight for distinguishing variation and peripheral movements. You must also prevent directly looking under the high illumination for seeing aura around the body for it has a little light. There are three kinds of cone cells; each of them will give ultimate response to only one of three main colors (red, green, and blue).

Each type is sensitive to a different range of wavelengths with maximums corresponding to 570 nm (red), 535 nm (green), and 445 nm (blue). In addition, there is a chemical material (rhodopsin) in rods with the ultimate light absorption of 505 nm; rods are composed of a protein and a special kind of vitamin A attached. The function of light-sensitive materials in cones and rods is almost the same. We discuss the function of rhodopsin here.

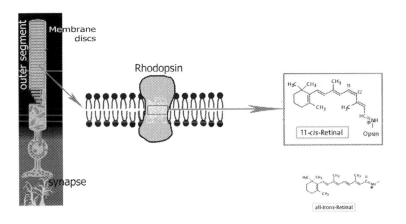

Rhodopsin is shaped by forming a connection between a kind of vitamin A (11-cis-retinal) and scotopsin (protein). When the light collides with rhodopsin, the retinal zone absorbs the light and a connection between 11-cis-retinal and scotopsin is broken. It makes rhodopsin active, so it decomposes to metarhodopsin. Then 11-cis-retinal changes into all-trans-retinal, which is not sensitive to light at all; the transfiguration is accompanied by some sort of enzyme, and chemical chain reactions stimulate bipolar cells. Bipolar cells establish synaptic connections to the other kinds of nervous cells, or so-called ganglion cells. The axons of ganglion cells converge as they leave the eyes as an optic nerve. During this chemical cycle, again, all-trans-retinal reshapes 11-cis-retinal; thus, they will be able to be combined with scotopsin. Consequently, rhodopsin will recover. This process makes photoreceptors inactive for a short time and they lose their sensitivity to light. It is known as photoreceptor compatibility.

Photoreceptors are made of two sections: inner and outer segments. The inner segment pumps sodium ions continuously to the outside of the cell. This causes negative potential differentiation in the cell.

Conversely, the outer segment, which is toward the retina and is exposed to the light, is penetrable to sodium ions in darkness. Hence, sodium ions with a positive electrical charge will penetrate into the cells and neutralize the negative charge of the cells. When rhodopsin of the outer segment is exposed to the light, it begins to decompose, and this will reduce the conductivity of sodium ions from the outer segment. Therefore, the number of exported ions from the inner segment becomes greater than imported sodium ions to the outer segment. This produces a negative charge in the cells, which in turn stimulates the nerves.

The stronger the radiated light, the more rhodopsin will be decomposed there. Thus, penetrability of the external membrane in relation to sodium ions will reduce. This increases the number of negative ions up to its ultimate degree—eighty millivolts—compared to the outer part of the cell.

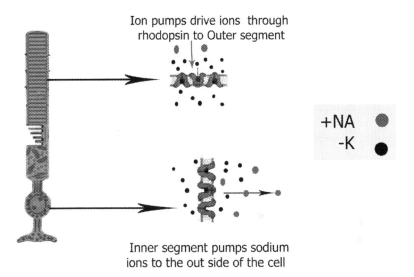

Ion pumps drive ions through
rhodopsin to Outer segment

+NA
-K

Inner segment pumps sodium
ions to the out side of the cell

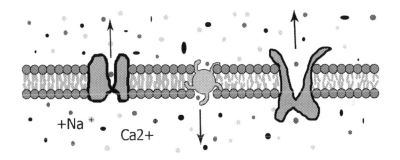

+Na +

Ca2+

After entering the darkness, sensitivity of the retina will increase
10 times after one minute, 6,000 times after twenty minutes, and
125,000 times after forty minutes.

The human brain is able to compensate for this deficiency by
continuous movements of the eyes as a small steady fluctuation.
When a cell becomes compatible with the light, it interchanges with
another cell, which is still sensitive to light, until the rest duration
(dark state) finishes.

Elimination of this fluctuation annihilates eyesight. Of course, if the speed of these movements becomes faster than the specified range, images will lose their clarity. Precisely, an image should be completely fixed for a short period in order to make synaptic connections between photoreceptors and neurons possible. Indeed, our eyes act as a camera that transforms fixed images to the brain; consequently, the brain makes a moving picture by attaching these images together.

The eyes give us three kinds of information from the environment:

1. The colors of objects, which in fact illustrate their different atomic structures
2. Volume, shape, location, and solidity of things
3. Spatial dimensions and size

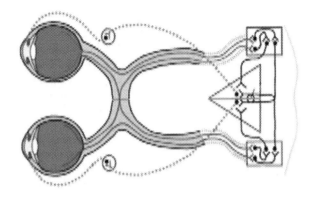

A. Color of Objects

One of the foundations and origins of the world's beauty is color. Color gives meaning to our life; in addition, it excites our feelings and brings variety to our life. We make ourselves up by colors; people believe that each color has its own specific interpretation.

Color even has entered into the metaphysical realm and has found a special place among its believers up to the extent that they consider it heavenly. You can see how perceptions of the optic channel have grounded our beliefs' foundations related to our lives and how they have overshadowed our knowledge and judgments. Have you ever asked yourself what the nature of color is or whether it is real or not?

Light is a form of energy. The unique characteristics of each photon are its wavelength and energy quantity; these are the only determinants which specify which of sensitive cells are to be stimulated and send nervous signals as the photon makes contact with photoreceptors. This organization in retina cells is due to the essence of chemical matter that exists in all kinds of photoreceptors. In fact, depending on the type of the cell which sends signals as well as the intensity of these signals, the brain will put a virtual label on it. In this manner, it perceives received signals transmitted by cone cells, which are sensitive to 430 nm, 540 nm, and 575 nm—blue, green, and red, in turn. This means that the energy which is needed for stimulation and initiation of a chemical action and reaction in photoreceptors—and, subsequently, in neurons—differs. Each cell only responds to a certain rate of energy, so light only provides the necessary energy for photoreceptors. It has nothing to do directly with color. In fact, colors are labels which our brain uses to detect the type of stimulated cell; they do not exist beyond our mind. Photoreceptors work as heat sensors and each of them is sensitive to a specific rate of energy. Moreover, the brain defines a distinguished color label for each group of sensors, and based on its definitions, it detects and separates different energy rates. In spite of the same nature of the waves, our brain perceives each of them as a unique color.

Visible light, which we are able to see, is confined to four hundred to seven hundred nanometers, which is only a small portion of a vast range of electromagnetic waves. These waves are too highly expanded to imagine; they just differ in rate of energy, frequency, and wavelength while they are similar in the nature of energy from which they are made of.

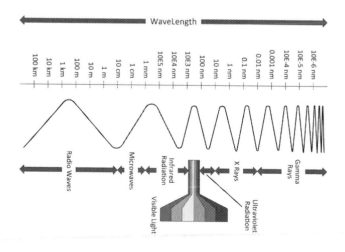

The energy rate of electromagnetic waves is obtained from the equation $E = hf$, where
E = wave energy
f = wave frequency
h = Planck's constant

Thus, the more the energy, the less the wavelength would be and vice versa. Therefore, if we suppose that energy has color, all electromagnetic waves, due to their similar nature, should have one unique color. However, it becomes lighter or darker due to the variation of energy quantity. What we actually observe is a collection of unique colors, of which they are not alike at all. Our brain then uses this sensory label, so-called color, in order to recognize wave energy differences better.

Molavi, in the sixth book of the *Masnavi*, says that discoloration is the essence and truth of all colors.

- Color does not exist.
- This is a discovery.
- This is a revelation of reality. It does not imply that no one had ever known this fact, but it shows that no one had ever noticed it and do not consider it for knowing himself.
- What we see as a world is completely different from what goes on outside of our minds.
- What we see is a mirage in wakefulness; there is no color in the world!

The credibility of our beliefs, logic, and judgments are dependent on the information we receive via our sense channels. Even the fundamentals of our reasoning are based on our faith in these senses, whereas they are not real! Honestly, our logic has been based on illusion for many years. Now you must have found out the reason I have initiated self-knowledge from sense inspection. Do not judge until you reach to the last page. Many schools, directly or indirectly, have pointed to this subject. However, who cares?

In the Quran (the holy book), life is called a "game" in this world.

"You don't even know what will happen tomorrow. What is your life? It is a mist that appears for a little while. Then it disappears" (James 4:14, the Bible).

Don Juan Matus introduces the world as a dream of our mind. According to him, the world is a dream which has been created in our mind as the result of our beliefs.

In mystical literature, we have the following:

I asked the condition of the world from a wise man.
He said, "It is an illusion, a dream, or a legend."
"Tell me the states of my life," I said.
"It is a flash, a candle, or a butterfly," he said.
"Why these people have attached to it?" I said.
"They are drunk, blind, or mad," he said.

Meanwhile, there is a profound relationship between colors and our psychic state. We discuss some of them here:

Dark blue: deep feeling, domination, self-determination, and a sensitive nature

Green: stability, stamina, inclination, pride, and ambition

Red: enthusiasm for living, great desires, bravery, goodwill, jealousy, animosity, sexual passion, and worry

Yellow: hope to solve problems, self-praising, fond of praise, hates criticism, dependent, activity and changeability, unfounded expectations, happy, and cheerful

Black: indifferent to life, disproving of everything, pessimism, doubt, obstinacy, denial of self, disregarding, surrender, and giving up

The one who chooses black wants to deny everything because he feels that everything is not what it should be.

WHY DO THINGS HAVE A FIXED COLOR?

The reflection of light from materials looks like a ball, which is sent back from a wall toward us. This implies the existence of a barrier in a distinguished distance from us that causes such reflection without giving any information about the color or the other characteristics of the barrier. The reflection of collided light waves from an object's surface acts as a bridge, which is the only connection between distant things and us. This reflection draws a shadow from dimensions and appearances of the objects in our retina without displaying their natures, colors, and details. Please pay attention to the following picture:

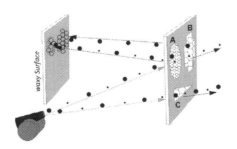

As you can see in the figure above, some pellets with a diameter of 2 and 3 cm are thrown turn by turn toward three netting barriers—A, B, and C—with hole dimensions of 1, 2.7, and 3.3 cm, respectively. As soon as they make contact with netting A, all pellets return to the waxy surface with a definite angle due to the small size of the netting holes. The collisions create a virtual image of netting on the waxy surface, which expresses its overall appearance. Due to the larger holes of netting B, the smaller pellets pass through, whereas it just reflects the larger pallets. In addition, netting C reflects none of them. That is why the waxy surface does not show any image of netting C.

In nature, different materials act as netting in which their atom characteristics determine the size of pores. Molecular arrangement is like netting and light acts as a pellet as well. The shorter the wavelength is, the bigger its power of penetrability will be. Thus, it can penetrate materials better and go through them (e.g., an X-ray). The longer the wavelength is, the smaller the power of its penetrability is. Waves are either absorbed or reflected. In other words, each object, due to its constant atom type and molecular arrangement, always reflects definite wavelengths. Consequently, the established nerve signals are always fixed and the brain uses color sensory labels in order to detect and classify received signals precisely.

Seeing does not occur in the eyes; eyes just are the means to translate reflected waves received from objects into nerve signals. Then our brain processes these signals in multiple points. There is no physical contact with light rays or objects. This abolishes any idea of similarity regarding the nature of colors between internal and external worlds.

In 1915, Albert Einstein, by introducing his famous formula, $E = mc^2$ explained the relationship between matter and energy, where

E = energy

m = mass

c = speed of light (300,000 km/sec)

He proved that matter is nothing but energy in its compressed form and is apparently static—like a hurricane, which is apparently a static form of wind, with dimensions more definite than the passing wind.

The wind does not stay in one place by its movement, but a hurricane fills up definite space due to its circular movement and spinning. It seems motionless in spite of moving forward.

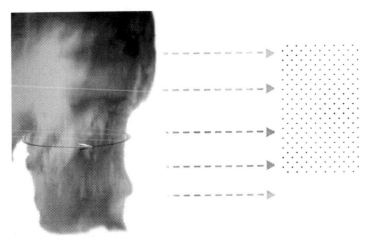

The unity in the structure of matter and energy implies that light and matter are alike in nature and our world is filled up with energy. Energy and matters are two sides of a coin. Energy has appeared in diversified forms in such a way that our brain takes these forms as matter and solid objects.

We float in an ocean of energy while we are a part of it; we are a constant and continuous part of this ocean, like a piece of ice floating in the water, whereas there is no difference between ice and water. The ice has preserved the totality of its own as an independent part. Actually, ice is a fraction of water molecules that can preserve the connection between its components and creates an independent collection out of water.

If we could see the molecules of water and ice, we would see that some of them have arranged a distinguished form in a definite place, though the connection between ice and water molecules has not been destroyed. In other words, you will see ice as a continuation of water and vice versa.

Comparable to ice, we are a pile of energy as well that has preserved our continuity in this ocean of energy while we are part of it. Let me put it in this way: We are the continuation of the being and being is the continuation of us.

We have made a solid and colorful world within ourselves out of a colorless ocean. Each of us observes our inner world as a bubble floating in this endless ocean.

Beings use unreal sensory labels in order to distinguish the differences between numbers and arrangements of energy fields in one collection. We perceive a colorful and charming world out of a colorless ocean of energy.

To give an example, consider iron and oxygen; the only difference between them is the number of consisting particles, not the nature of the particles. Iron is made of fifty-six energy fields in the center (protons and neutrons) and twenty-six other fields (electrons) that are spinning around. Oxygen has sixteen energy fields in the center and eight particles around the center. Suppose we have put fifty-six bricks and sixteen bricks of the same nature in different places. Is it right to say the first collection is completely different from the other one? It is more interesting that we perceive each collection with different colors, smells, and tastes!

Living creatures are living in their own mental world during their life span. They have nothing in common save for a few details. People try to describe their own realities related to universe based on their own perception, description, and inner mentality. The existing universe lacks any smell, taste, color, darkness, voice, and solidity. All these are attributes which belong to the world inside beings. Considering perceptual memory differences and structural variations among them, each creature owns its unique world. The creatures' perceptual worlds, like themselves, do not have any similarities!

Feelings via beings' senses cannot be explained. Moreover, people cannot perceive any other feelings aside from their own feelings, except those that can be understood in comparison with their preceding memory.

Meanwhile, words act as a covering which hides the perception gap among human beings. We have to put names on things and constant motives in order to point them out whenever we converse. In this way, we recall common memories in each other's minds. For instance, the wavelength of red is seven hundred nanometers. Indeed, the word *red* does not refer to a color; rather, it is the name of wavelength with seven hundred nanometers. As we hear the word, we refer to our memory related to the specific wave.

The question is whether our memories of colors or waves are alike. Do we all see red the same? Either we use one common title, red, for our different memories. Unless it is not built by our mind, the light lacks of color. Is it possible to see it with different colors?

Colors are traces of waves in creatures' brains, while such words like *red, blue*, etc., are the names of waves, not the effect of them. It means that these names are titles we conventionally put on different wavelengths of light, whereas color—apart from the name itself—is an influence caused by light since a unique wave can create different effects. It depends on different parameters such as structure, quality, kind of interpretation, and nature of the interpreter or transformer.

Perceptional memories cannot transform into words. If it were possible, we could explain color for color-blind people. In fact, we use words to refer to common wavelengths. As soon as one hears "red," the listeners call back the memory of the wave to their minds; nevertheless, no one can claim to understand the speaker's perceptions of red. If the listener does not have any tangible memory related to the motive, they cannot understand it and will try to simulate it with preceding memories.

Beings compare everything with their perceptual memories. That is why they are not able to understand others. Their internal worlds are too far from each other that no one can conceive it at all. We think we understand each other while the truth is that we are completely different. The sky may be blue in one's world while it is red in the other person's world. These differences have been hidden due to a common language and conventions among society. Actually, the nature of feelings does not allow them to be translated into words.

For example, a raven sees black, silver, and white—graphite as well. A honeybee can see the ultraviolet light reflected from the bottom of any azure flower, while it is not able to see the color red. A dog perceives the world black and white due to lack of cone cells in its retina. Some other animals can only see moving things. Thus, they must move their head in order to observe motionless objects.

Normally, human beings are not able to understand the perception of a bee or raven; hence, they think that animals see the world like them. Sometimes people of different genders, both male and female, think they are close to each other and completely understand each other. A female is in favor of roughness, being soothed, harshness, dignity, and power of her spouse, while a man is the opposite. He hates even thinking about having a baby in his stomach, contrary to woman. Even in a sexual relationship between a man and a woman, which is one of the important factors of their coexistence, their perceptions are so far from each other to the extent that none of them wants to be in the other one's place.

Sensetivity	Lamp's color C	Sensetivity	Lamp's color B	Sensetivity	Lamp's color A	Room No.
30 V	Yellow	20 V	Red	10 V	Blue	1
30 V	Blue	20 V	Yellow	10 V	Red	2
30 V	Red	20 V	Blue	10 V	Yellow	3

Imagine a lake with three rooms deep inside it. They are completely insulated and stimuli cannot attach to them due to their insulators. In each room, three lamps with blue, red, and yellow colors are attached to an antenna via an electric circuit, which is sensitive to electrical fluctuation.

These lamps are arranged in such a way that each of them is sensitive to ten, twenty, or thirty volts according to the following table.

There is a person in each room. These people do not know each other's language. They are supposed to let the other rooms know the color they see as they receive electric signals. Now if we enter ten volts of power in the lake, the lamps of each room will be illuminated and each one will see the color that conforms to the lamp number.

In order to exchange received signals with each other, these people have to use conventional and fixed labels for each voltage. For instance, they choose green for the ten-volt lamp, dark blue for the twenty-volt lamp, and black for the thirty-volt lamp.

Then for expressing illumination of lamp A, they inform each other that they observe a green color. However, the person in charge of the room 1 thinks what is called green is blue. A person in room 2 considers green as red; also, the same thing occurs in the third room. They are not able to distinguish the perception gap unless they can find their way to each other's rooms.

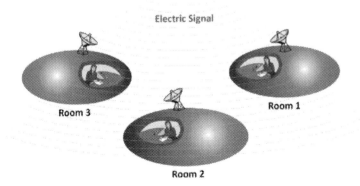

Electric Signal

Room 3

Room 1

Room 2

Like the aforementioned example, words are conventional and hide beings, whereas received motives are common. Thus, words can cause the perception differences to be maintained forever.

Shall we keep quarrelling with people who do not understand us! Perhaps we must find another solution for communication.

Light and Luminance

Light is one of the mystical words, both in the physics and metaphysics realms.

Light has a particular position in human beliefs to the extent that we consider holy things with illuminated appearances as well as relate darkness to impurity and dirtiness.

When one photon of a visible band of light collides with a dust particle, its density and momentum are so small in comparison with the particle's mass that it does not make any changes in its condition.

After contact, the static particle remains motionless, and if it is moving, the photon is not able to stop it. It resembles, in comparison, a mosquito and a huge rock. Thus, a photon's contact with a particle in elastic form, in which the photon springs back, passes through a microscopic optic system and reaches our eyes.

However, an electron is another particle. We can waiver its mass in comparison with the mass of dust particles and their momentum; even at light speed, it is too low. In this condition, we send gamma ray photons toward it; their momentum is almost one hundred milliard times greater than the momentum of an electron. Thus, there would be no trace of the electron after the clash.

Hence, the idea of taking an image of an electron—or at least dark and bright strips—fails. This recalls the clash of a gigantic airplane with a pigeon in the air.

Now we choose a motionless electron. We know its speed is zero, but we do not know where it is. We look for it with gamma rays. However, at the time of clash, the electron will be thrown to a far corner of space; and no one knows where the gigantic shooter has thrown it.

But in an ordinary microscope we do not have a problem with dust particles or bacteria, and we can determine their location and speed easily, whereas if one tries to find the location of the electron, it is impossible to get information about its speed because it will be thrown to a far, inaccessible point. Conversely, if one tries to find its speed, its location will be changed due to the impact.

The mass and size of an electron is far greater than that of light particles, and it is still invisible, let alone light particles that have nearly zero mass. Of course, we cannot see them. In fact, what we see and call light is due to stoppage of light in the retina. Light cannot touch the luminance perception zone, and what we perceive is nothing but the result of nervous stimulation and receiving signals from optic nerves.

In a completely dark room without any visible light, close your eyes and push your hands on your eyes. Luminance will appear. In spite of the absence of light, a visible wavelength, you will see something, which we know of as false light (photon). Only pressure from your hands has stimulated the optic channel and yet you mistakenly call this feeling and perception of the brain about these nerve signals "light."

This experience reveals that whenever optic nerves are stimulated by light or any other motive, something appears in perception that is mistakenly called light (photon). There is no need for visible waves to see luminance before our eyes; actually, every other motive which incites the eyes can create luminance.

The other reason for our inability to see light (photon) itself is that in order to see the volume, dimension, and overall appearance of something, some particles that are far smaller than the object must contact it. Afterward, they must be reflected so that they can make out the outline and dimensions of the object in the retina; since there is no particle (or wave) smaller than the photon, the establishment of an image of light in the retina will not be possible. Look at the following picture:

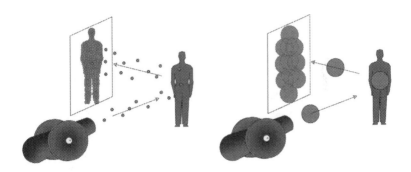

As you can see, the smaller the collided particles are, the more precise the created image is. Conversely, if the dimensions of particles become bigger than object, the image would be ambiguous and meaningless. That is why scientists are incapable of seeing particles such as protons or electrons, let alone photons.

Luminance, darkness, color, and solidity are all part of our perceptional dreams about external realities. Here the question is whether the external world is as bright or dark as our inner world is. What is the essence of the luminance we see in the world? Is it just the result of our interpretations and our perceptional dreaming? It seems the brightness which we perceive means we observe our environment more clearly and more lucidly as well.

Light is neither bright nor dark; it is only light. It is only an entity, only corpuscular particle or wave. In addition, the existing universe is neither bright nor dark, but within ourselves, we make it bright or dark. If we are not capable of perceiving something through our senses, we could make it detectable by comparing it with our previous perceptional memories. Since we do not have any memory of a third state that is neither dark nor bright, we are incapable of understanding it.

In fact, this form of perception is created via beings' mutual communication with an existing universe. Thus, no one can claim to know what the world really looks like. Here this is the other interesting fact about the faultiness of messages received from optic channel!

This is a magical story about the differences between what is inside creatures' brains and what is going on beyond their minds.

Think about your beliefs. To what extent has the belief of luminance instead of light formed your faith? When you think of God, angels, immaterial universes, etc., to what extent has your concept of light influenced those concepts?

Unfortunately, because of his ignorance—in all times—human beings have directly related light to terms such as *God*, *spirit*, and so forth. He has mistaken it for luminance in his mind and has even ranked holy beings and universes according to brightness or darkness; also, he has applied luminance to imagine them.

Do not mistake and do not judge as you always do! You know nothing about the meaning of light mentioned in divine religions. The light pointed out in holy books is not photonic. Indeed, it means "what makes things appear" or "discloser." A photon is also known as light because it makes things visible. Thus, the phrase "God is the light of heavens and the earth" (الله نور السموات و الارض)—which is the description of God in the holy Quran—or "This is the message we have heard from and proclaim to you, that God is light and in him is no darkness at all" (1 John 1:5, the Bible) does not mean that God is the luminance of the heavens and the earth; it implies that God is the discloser (light) of the heavens and the earth. Likewise, the luminance dignities of the world are applied to the extent that facts are revealed in the world.

Luminance—likewise, colors—is just confined to a creature's inner world and it does not exist in the real world in a way that we perceive. Since we do not have any other memory of light except brightness and darkness from childhood up to now, we are incapable of perceiving the third state, which is what light really is.

How could we rely on our beliefs if their foundations are based on interpretations of our senses? Some people have intuition of colorful or luminous scenes. Are they reliable? Is it possible to know God without knowing ourselves?

Color does not exist. Darkness does not exist. Luminance does not exist. Beings do not see a unique object with unique color. Each being has its own internal world—and human beings!

B. VOLUME, SHAPE,
AND SOLIDITY OF OBJECTS

When you look at the environment around you and see different forms and their solidity, you assume they are full of material and their forming particles are settled side by side in compressed form. However, what we see which our tactile sense affirms is an unreal volume of things.

All materials and elements from the wall to our bodies are made of small particles called atoms. These atoms, in turn, are made of smaller particles called protons, neutrons, and electrons. In fact, atom is the name applied to the collection of these three particles. Protons and neutrons are placed in atom's center, and electrons—with the nearly 1/1800 mass of a proton—are spinning around the atomic nucleus.

The distance between the nucleus and the first orbital of electrons in relation to the volume of an atom is to the extent that if we magnify the nucleus diameter to the size of a hazelnut, the distance between electron and nucleus would be half a kilometer. However, the fast spinning of electrons around the nucleus—near or at light speed—causes the atom to exhibit an unreal volume of itself. (We prefer to use simple models considering the fact that the aim of this book is to be simple, and in this discussion, we would have the same result from all atomic models.)

If we tie a luminous ball to one end of a rope and begin to rotate the rope at a fast speed, it would seem like a big loop of fire instead of a luminous point. This illusion arises from an optic channel deficiency which photographs objects and things at a low cycling rate compared to electron spinning speed.

When light radiates on the retina, it creates a chain of chemical reactions in photoreceptors which makes cells inactive for a short period. After engaging complicated chemical reactions, which leads to excitation of optic nerves, cells return to their preceding condition and regain their sensitivity to the light—exactly similar to a capacitor, which needs a temporal pause after each discharge in order to recharge again. This inactivity of retina cells—in spite of continuous movement of retina cells, which prevents abnormality of vision—makes us take pictures of events with a distinguished cycling rate; our brain creates a moving picture in perception through the connecting of these photos like movie camera. This process is the main reason of vision faultiness during seeing moving things, especially in high speed. Pay attention to the picture below:

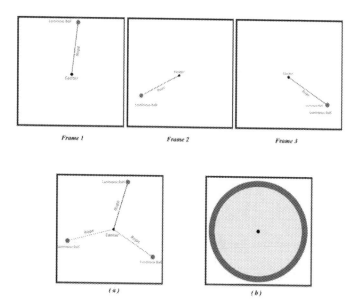

In this picture, the eyes take three photos, in three frames, and dispatch it to the brain. Receiving these three photos, the brain compares them and concludes that the center of all photos coincides.

Because of constant size of the rope and the coincidence of the pictures' centers in all three images, the brain detects the type and path of movement so it rebuilds it like image A, and along with conjoining all following pictures, creates the path of the luminous ball as a virtual image as you see in picture B.

It implies that instead of seeing the luminous ball, our brain defines its motion field as a bulk solid and colorful space and shows it for our perception. In other words, instead of seeing fluctuated particles, we observe the path of their movement in a huge space, which seems like a solid area. In fact, objects and materials around us are virtual images which our mind has built up via observing a moving field of very small particles. The wall, more than being a wall, is an image of a moving space.

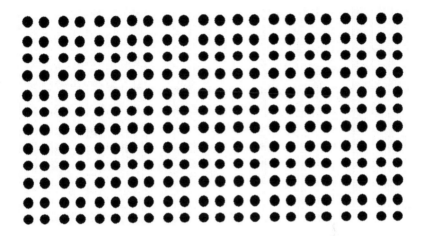

As mentioned before, some animals' eyes lack the vibration. That is why they are not capable of seeing motionless things and materials unless they move or things become mobile.

In picture F, you see adjoining atoms of matter, which seems solid and spherical due to fluctuation of its fundamental particles. In fact, these balls are virtual images built by movement of electrons.

The fast spinning speed of electrons around the nucleus causes us to see an atom as a solid ball; consequently, all elements and materials seem solid and bulky. If it were possible to compress all materials on the earth in such a way that all voids could omitted, the earth, as it transforms into a black hole, would be as big as a basketball. It shows that matter with such small volume has fluctuated in the space as big as the planet earth and has created a virtual image of this planet.

When you look at the wall, more than observing a solid material, you see an exhibition performed by electrons due to their fast speed, and you perceive these motion paths as a wall full of material.

Universe is universe, since our eyes are imperfect, and it goes on until we are imperfect. When our eyes become perfect and perceive the world perfectly, this world will completely collapse. Instead, an ocean of energy will appear with small particles floating through it; the flow of waves draws these particles out to every direction.

In contrary to our conception, things and materials are not bulky and solid. Solidity is a dream and a memory which is built by our mind. It is made of small material which is formed in a vast space, just like a TV screen in which only one point lights up. This point moves within the entire screen at a fast speed. It creates beautiful moving images via turning off and on or becoming darker and brighter in different places of the TV screen.

If electrons stop fluctuating once, everything will disappear. In fact, we are observers of an imaginary world that an electron, like a painter, has portrayed skillfully for us regarding imperfection of the optic channel. Moreover, our perception has beautified it by its charming colors in order to make us believe what we see is a real world.

Undoubtedly, anything which cannot be interpreted by this dream or anything which cannot be seen in our imaginary world is incredible and unacceptable. What we name universe is a wide 3-D screen in which electrons are performing by their fluctuation. We observe a virtual image and the effect of electrons' movement, which does not exist beyond our mind! The universe is colorless and hollow. Movement governs it. The information received via the optic channel cannot be a proper reference for our beliefs, judgments, and real knowledge of the universe; surely, no gained perceptional memories based on this information will be reliable.

In our inner world, the speed of each event is different from what really goes on outside of us. In fact, we ourselves define speed for events and these speeds are not real.

Suppose that a bullet is fired with a speed of 500 m/s from a gun while, every 50 meters, it rotates 180 degrees around itself. Simultaneously, two cameras, A and B, with a speed of fifty frames per second, record this event and send it to a processor. One processor with a speed of twenty frames per second (C) and the other with a speed of five hundred frames per second (D) processes and receives information. Now what will happen?

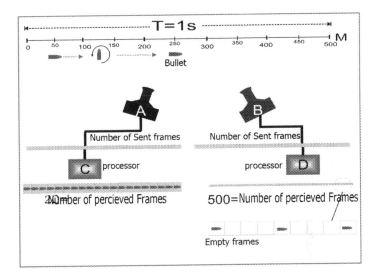

Events that happened between two frames are hidden to both cameras. In the output of both cameras, there is no sign of the 180-degree bullet rotation.

In processor C, many images will be omitted due to decreased speed of processing relative to the camera; hence, some events will be discarded and bullet movement seems faster than its actual speed.

In this state, the observer will see the bullet movement as glittering luminous line. Thus, the observer will see an illusion. This implies that instead of seeing a moving bullet, he sees a luminous line.

In processor D, many frames will remain empty between every two images due to higher speed of processing relative to the camera; thus, bullet movement seems slower with a delay. It seems that the bullet stops at each moment and goes on again. We will see more details of the bullet in this state, but what is perceived is not the actual speed and method of movement.

From a time-place point of view, the speed of the bullet relative to both cameras is the same. Processors perceive each processed frame as one unit of inner time; thus, the processors perceive the speed of the bullet far differently from each other. It seems that they are alive during the process and dead during the interval between two frames. However, when observers talk about the bullet's speed, they both mention a numerical unique speed due to using similar time and place equations.

According to the definitions, by saying one second, we mean the time that lasts for a bullet in order to go from point x to x1 without considering perceived duration due to observer. In fact, time is of elastic quality and varies from one observer to another. In other words, the greater the speed of processing is, the more partial the perceived time is, and time will feel longer from an observer's point of view.

Our eyes are not able to see continuously, but they take photos in the form of frames; that is to say, they are inactive between two frames. Our brain, which consists of a complicated conjunction of neurons, also processes received information from the eyes with constant speed and builds a moving picture.

It implies that between intervals of this alternation, the brain is completely off, like someone who is conscious for ten minutes conscious and then unconscious for ten minutes. However, he does not realize it due to the fast speed between becoming conscious and becoming unconscious. Thus, he cuts the intervals between frames and perceives flow of frames.

We see the wall because the speed of an electron is faster than our eyes' photographing and our brain's processing. If our brain and our eyes were as fast as electrons and if our eyes were able to see particles with a dimension of one electron pixel, the universe would have vanished and would have been replaced with a colorless and turbulent ocean of energy.

Even if the speed of taking pictures and the brain's processing were doubled, the movement of objects would decrease to half of what it is and the day would last forty-eight hours without encountering our equations regarding velocity and time.

We only perceive a fraction of time, of which we take a photo. Moreover, time expands according to our processing speed that will be discussed in detail in the book *Time*.

Likening life to a mirage in diversified religions and speeches of the great men of literature and mysticism indicates that human beings became aware of this matter a long time ago.

In fact, this earthly life is nothing but a plaything:[3] "إِنَّمَا الْحَيَاةُ الدُّنْيَا لَعِبٌ وَلَهْوٌ"—the description of God in the holy Quran."

World is always the same as long as we believe it because we know how to hold its images; consequently, if one drops his unreal beliefs about those images, the world collapses.[4]

We are floating in an endless ocean of energy; like a bulb, we have dedicated our destiny to the turbulence of these waves. Imperfection and deficiency of our perception outlets build a charming mirage from this ocean within ourselves, which we then observe—a mirage which, due to its steady nature, has gone deep into our being with the passing of time in a way that we count it as the most real subject of our life. Thus, on this basis, we start building our dreams, hopes, targets, pains, despairs, faith, and beliefs, and interpret anything regarding this. Therefore, we assume that whatever is in contradiction to it is meaningless and superstitious while our present artificial world is the biggest mirage; also, it is the biggest masterpiece of existence as well.

---

3   Quran 47:36
4   Don Juan Matus, *The Second Ring of Power*

C. Spatial Dimensions of Things and Size

The third part of received information via optic channel is the dimension and space that forms length, width, and height in our inner world and enables us to distinguish distance. It gives depth to our mental images. Detection of dimensions via optic channel is accomplished by two methods:

A. Via optic lens alteration and superposing of two received images from the eyes

B. Via memories, experiences, and definitions we acquire gradually through the relation between image lines and their location (with the help of the tactile channel)

The human being is a cognitive creature that has missed the point that his corporeal being is only and only a complicated chemical system. Factually, this machine calls what it builds inside the "world" and establishes sciences such as mathematics and philosophy based on these perceptions.

"Dimensions" are included among such perceptions. Dimensions are established via our optic channel and with the help of our tactile channel. Have you ever thought about what would happen in the absence of the tactile channel and its assistance for interpreting optical information?

What is known as a dimension in physics consists of directions in which a particle is allowed to expand. This expansion in our inner world happens in three directions—length, width, and height—in assistance with optic channel, which forms volume and three-dimensional space. Lack of cooperation between these two senses in perceiving space and dimension would omit our understanding of time and place.

With the elimination of the tactile sense, we would not be able to feel our body volume, which is in fact our body expansion in three-dimensional space. In this case, depth, space, volume, movement, and distance will lose their meaning, and we will not be able to distinguish the space between objects and ourselves. Here, it is good to know that there is a difference between lack of the tactile sense and insensibility, paralysis, and unfeelingness of an organ.

Since, in a state of unfeelingness, tactility exists but does not receive any message from its surroundings or a specific organ, it is still possible for us to simulate it and recall its preceding memories. While on the case of our tactile channel's elimination, not only can we not feel our body, but we would also lose perceptional memories relative to that channel since recalling those memories requires the tactile sense itself, just as opening a 3ds Max or PDF file and reading its information makes it necessary to install related software on the computer. Otherwise, these files remain as an unreadable and meaningless pack of information.

Hence, in the case of tactile sense elimination, we would not be able to simulate or recall our preceding memories of this sense. We would then imagine our entire visionary field as one point which could not be separated from "me," whereas it also does not belong to "me."

If, suddenly, the tactile sense is omitted, we would not even realize its elimination. Without feeling anything, we continue living since our memories of the tactile sense would not be readable by our perception. In this case, we would not have any memory of the past regarding this sense to compare our present with what has been in the past. Actually, everything would lose its expansion and dimension would be omitted.

Distance would be meaningless and movement would lose its concept. Hot and cold, softness and roughness—all would be meaningless, and we would not understand solidity, volume, movement, and size.

In these circumstances, what would happen to your present beliefs? What examples would the holy books resort to describe the afterworld?

In fact, each part of our inner world originated from one sense, and sensorial channels (optic, auditory, olfactory, taste, and tactile) are instruments that we utilize for perceiving and communicating with the universe. Properties, rules, shapes, and dimensions in our world originated from our senses. In other words, we have formed the world and, hence, have attributed properties to it and these properties have nothing to do with the real world.

For instance, no object can pass through a wall or travel through distances without time passing or without displacement. All of these are the rules and properties that our senses have imposed on our inner world and cause us to take what we perceive as real rules and properties of the existing universe.

In diversified religions and throughout history, these rules have been broken by many examples.

- Floating through the air and overcoming the earth's gravity
- Displacement of objects and even human beings without traveling through space or time
- Stories of holy books like the Quran (e.g., in the case of bringing the queen of Sheba's throne from a far distance in just a moment)
- Disappearance of Don Juan in front of his disciple, Castaneda
- Miracles of prophets and mystics

All of them are examples in which common rules of humanity have been broken.

Solidity, dimension, space, volume, and their related laws are some of these forms and properties. What prevents us from passing through the wall is not the wall itself, but our tactile channel, the part which human beings developed physical theories for without considering the environment. With tactility lacking, our realization of the universe would be different from what it is now, and there would not be such physical laws and theories.

Now in this case, imagine what the scientists' point of view would be. What would happen to physics and mathematics laws? What about our detectors and machines—could they assist us to perceive space and dimensionality? Then solid and solidity would lose their meanings—and also the heat and coolness and our present body.

In fact, the wonders are nothing but changing of one's internal definitions about the world in profound perceptual and emotional levels of the subconscious mind domain.

Dimension is an image and illusion of the outer environment, which our mind constructs with the assistance of the optic and tactile channels in the form of continuum or space. We have created dimension in our inner world and then expanded it in three directions—length, width, and height—in a way that, in normal conditions, we are not able to perceive more or less dimensions since we have been learned to see, think, and believe three-dimensionally.

Despite the fact that dimensions are spawned by our mind, we are naturally unable to imagine more or less dimensions. We cannot understand length and width in the absence of a third dimension in spite of being in our perception zone. We cannot think two-dimensionally. What we apparently see as two-dimensional (e.g., a surface) is placed in three-dimensional coordinates and is in accordance with a three-dimensional environment and a two-dimensional surface is understandable for us only when it is placed in a three-dimensional environment.

It is not possible to perceive lower dimensions in an environment with higher dimensions and vice versa. A world that lacks any form of height is not imaginable for us and even the most intelligent human is unable to realize it since he does not have any preceding memory of it and all their memories are limited to surroundings with length, width, and height.

Two-dimensional perceptions necessitate imagining yourself as two-dimensional. A body without height and a world without depth are not imaginable. If the universe had two dimensions, we would be unable to perceive and even realize a third dimension. Thus, an extensive part of existence would not be accessible for our perception, and we would not be able to observe the present world and many creatures, objects, and shapes. Certainly, rules of physics, mathematics, geometry, philosophy, etc., were different from present rules, and equations, theories, knowledge, and experiences were unable to justify many events and phenomena. Furthermore, it would be impossible for us to accept three-dimensional creatures.

Similarly, unknowns and secrets would be more than they are now; the unknowns could not ever be answered as in order to solve their paradoxes it would be necessary to understand three-dimensional space.

Look at the picture below. Apparently, this picture that has two dimensions is only a simple scheme with meaningless coloring and twisted lines. However, a hidden shape within the picture is only perceivable in three-dimensional space.

To see a hidden three-dimensional shape in the picture, you must hold the page 40-50 centimeters away from your eyes and try to superpose two black points by crossing your eyes, and do not let it move from that point, then put your concentration on the image. After few minutes, a clear three-dimensional image will appear—a picture which can be seen only by adding another dimension to it; otherwise, it cannot exist.

Two senses, tactile and optic, together create space and distance. Then not only motion would be meaningful but also objects would be recognized as separate things. The picture above was somehow an example of this matter. Without giving depth to it via the senses, things inside the picture would not be separated and hence would not be understood. When the brain gives dimension to the mentioned picture by utilizing internal descriptions, space—along with things inside—will appear, and we observe a three-dimensional space with distinct objects.

We look at a surface as a two-dimensional image. Actually, our brain—based on definitions attained through time about lines, curves besides lens alteration, and highlights distribution plus memories of volume, expansion, distance, and motion—draws it in three-dimensional coordinates and then observes it. In addition, it creates a three-dimensional space in which a human head is placed while it does not exist in reality.

If we delete height from our world, geometrical shapes would be meaningless. In such a world, a circle, a rectangle, or a triangle would not be seen as they exist now with our three-dimensional coordinates. They would look like lines without thickness that have the same measure; when an observer looks perpendicular to each shape from different angles, they may become smaller or bigger. Moreover, other geometrical shapes would seem like lines with different lengths without any thickness. Thus, the differences, which are assumed among these figures in three-dimensional world, would not be meaningful in a two-dimensional world; thus, trigonometry rules cannot justify their relationships.

Can our olfactory and optic channels create or perceive more or less dimensions?

Do dimensions belong to the real world? Are nature and the shape of beings exactly what we see? Either that or many shapes in our universe are only products of our interpretations of the world. Are we able to see all aspects of the real world? Either that or we rebuild only chosen fragments, after filtration, within ourselves.

The presumption about the existence of nonorganics, other worlds, the afterworld, and eternity are some beliefs that human beings have been faithful to through time; they caused many wars. Do other beings exist that we are not capable of seeing due to diversified reasons? Are they invisible due to their dissimilar dimensions to our three-dimensional world? If we were able to see higher dimensions, would other forms of life be added to our world?

If we prepare a superficial slice, a two-dimensional surface, from a crowd of people and then give it to the well-known scientists of our age and ask them whether there is any human being in that place, they would make fun of us for sure. Since a created two-dimensional image is so different from reality, there is no explanation for it. You may think that the created image would look like picture 1, but you are wrong since atoms and electrons are not included in the horizontal slice.

In real sectioning, an atom would be cut too, so the probability of presence of electron, proton, and neutron in one surface simultaneously would amount to nearly zero. Thus, not all atoms and body components of an individual would appear on the surface.

Meanwhile, what you see in picture 1 is apparently a two-dimensional image of a section, but practically, what you see is a two-dimensional image in three-dimensional coordinates. In two-dimensional coordinates, such a shape is not visible. Thus, the created picture would look like picture 2 rather than picture 1. However, picture 2 is a three-dimensional image of a surface.

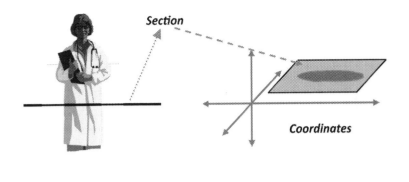

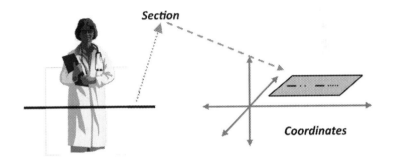

In picture 2, the derived shape is a sign of a creature which cannot be seen in the two-dimensional world; but it has left a trace of being somehow, so the perceiver will not be able to understand reality until it becomes three-dimensional.

We observe our inner world and we are not able to perceive the universe directly, but we rebuild the world, its objects, and beings in our sensorial forms via constructing perceptional forms; and we create their laws and relationships by this simulation, which is far removed from reality.

This causes the disappearance of many aspects of the universe as well as the looming of insubstantial images in our inner world. Perhaps many shapes and objects we see in our world are an incomplete trace of unknown creatures which have appeared in the form of stones, trees, birds, etc., due to their embedment in our three-dimensional world. Actually, what we see in our inner world, like picture 2, are incomplete sections of creatures and objects.

While studying heavenly books or mystical passages, you often come across some quotations that may seem completely meaningless, illogical, superstitious, and nonsensical.

Actually, when someone wants to translate his perceptions of the real world (the world without size, color, solidity, etc.) into the language of human beings' inner dreams, they are obliged to resort to the words and sciences of the present time. This makes it look imperfect in the next age. With the passing of time, sciences will be subjected to alteration as they become complete. The fact is that when a great master wants to translate his findings obtained by intuition to human language he must use words and expressions of his own time and since the science is progressing the master's saying seems to be incomplete in future, If a neurologist travels through time with a time machine and faces the greatest scientist of that time, how would he transfer his knowledge? Would he seem illiterate in that period? For in explaining his knowledge, he must be proficient in sciences and literature of that time in order to express his knowledge written in ancient words in an understandable way. Imperfectness of human knowledge in every era and word *deficiency* in explaining perceptions cause some words of men of knowledge to seem meaningless for ordinary people.

However, you must consider that all these words make deep sense for wise men that have become free from the slavery of words.

The optic channel—regarding the fact that the nearer the object is, the more convex the lens would be and vice versa—along with information that has been obtained through time due to lines and highlights plus perception of space which has been created by the tactile sense, forms two parameters of dimension and space within ourselves. Moreover, it provides a continuum for the presence of things and occurrences among them. This continuum and space give meaning to many concepts such as movement, distance, volume, etc. These definitions interpret components of the external world within ourselves and draw for us an illusive specter of what is outside.

What is a machine? What is the use of it and within what limits would it help us? Are they able to lead us beyond the boundary of our senses? To what extent can they do this if the answer is yes?

Our mistake is we think that, by expansion of our abilities in scientific fields—such as the detection of X-rays and gamma rays, taking pictures from microstructures, discovery of black holes, or detection of cosmic and radioactive rays—we have entered domains beyond our senses. Do not make a mistake! In such discoveries, we are not going beyond our senses, but we just amplify our senses' domains.

In addition, our machines only work as amplifiers or converters; they translate and convert stimuli to suit our perception boundaries. In fact, a machine is an instrument which is able to eliminate weaknesses of our body and senses in that same domain, not beyond it.

For instance, if we lacked an optic sense, we would not build a camera, and no machine, even if it could manifest the truth of light, could show the third state of light. That is because we build our machines in a way that their outputs are convertible to information or stimuli which we are able to perceive; finally, stimuli and output data of all machines enter the entrance of body structures (senses), and the same thing will happen to them.

If a machine made by a human could exhibit the world in four dimensions, we would see it in three dimensions since our optic sense, which is a biological device, is not able to perceive a fourth dimension. Moreover, the output data of all machines are interpreted by our channels the same way as other environmental stimuli, and our channels put sensorial labels on them.

No machine is able to exhibit for us the colorless external world. No device is able, and will not be able, to show us the third state of light and . . .

In my opinion, scientists, theoreticians, and philosophers are visionary people hallucinating in a confined circle. To justify their fanciful theories, they look for occurrences, experiences, and witnesses. However, sometimes a phenomenon or an experiment yields a predictable result, but it has been proven in history that after some time passes, another reason will be found for that same occurrence. In fact, as in Science Philosophy:

Science and philosophy are not discoveries of human beings of reality, but beautiful unstable imagination and inventions of humanity.

We are slaves

Eternal slaves

Slaves in cage of body and sense;

Enslaved by a dream, a vision, and a charming mirage;

Without any exit door;

Seeing is not a good reason for being and vice versa.

What do you expect from a detector machine or a measurement device?

Firstly, it must give us necessary information. However, the device is dependent and only carries out orders of human beings—a machine that looks through the world of small particles under our orders to reveal the structure of materials and bodies of organic beings; in fact, it is a mutual instrument. In other words, it has "initial" and "ending" or "input" and "output." Phenomena, which happen at the device input, are following the world's rules, whereas the output of machine speaks the language of our five senses since our sense academy is just familiar with this language.

We ask the device to give us precise data about the location, mass, material, size, quality, and velocity of a particle. It confesses sincerely that it is not able to do so; it can only distinguish some of these specifications since recognition of one parameter often causes another factor to remain unknown. Meanwhile, it mentions if it exhibits all aspects of a particle for us, we will not be able to understand and observe many of its aspects due to filtration, which we apply via perceptional channels.

For instance, we ask the device to show us the location and velocity of particle or exhibit all aspects of a particle. The machine will show all dimensions, but the observer only sees three of them. By the way, the device is not able to indicate the location and velocity of particle simultaneously and defines only one of them precisely since recognition of one of these quantities makes the particle to be thrown to faraway place.

Actually, we have made the device to apprehend the location and velocity of particle according to the customaries in classical physics and to give us a comprehensive report. However, an unpredictable fact is that there is no relationship between these two parameters and they are completely two independent quantities.

In 1927, Werner Heisenberg mentioned that, however, waves and materials can be equally related to atoms, but for defining them precisely, experiments must be done separately. Heisenberg proved that it is impossible to instantaneously measure position (x) and momentum ($p = mv$) of a material point on an x-axis with absolute certainty.

Measurement of these two at once is always made along with uncertainty. If we consider a measurement error of position x as Δp_x and momentum as Px, we will have $\Delta p_x \Delta x \geq h$.

We define this as such for our measurement devices to exhibit which parameters and in what form; this implies that our devices and our senses will not be able to perceive, detect, and calculate many parameters of universe for an eternity.

Our world is the product of our mental definitions. Hence, we are unable to see the reality of each creature. What appears in our inner world in three-dimensional form as objects and living creatures might be the trace of other creatures that have appeared in other shapes due to our inner world limitations and sense channel filtering. Thus, each thing in our world is not exactly what we see, but it might be presentation and sign of another being that has been appeared imperfectly in our world.

An image establishes itself two-dimensionally in the retina, and it is our brain that makes it three-dimensional by using its definitions of lines, darkness, illumination, and the cavity alteration of the eye lens. Besides, the tactile channel also confirms this image and keeps us away from knowing the reality of things.

In spite of being two-dimensional, our eyes perceive the above images three-dimensionally. In fact, what makes three-dimensional perception of images are the definitions we have learned from lines, highlights, and relative angles of shapes through time. This matter causes many errors. Examples are shown in the picture below:

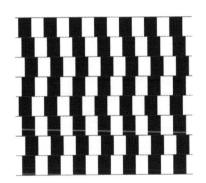 

We are observers of the world within our skull, and what we see is product of our mental interpretations from environmental stimuli based on perceptional memories. In fact, the real world is nonorganic relative to our inner world. If, one day, we could see the world without interpretations of perception, certainly, we would see things that are absent in our world now and we call them nonorganic.

Think about objects and beings that have appeared in our world in diversified forms. What are their real shapes? Creatures such as angels, devils, and demons—are they imaginary, or are they just covered due to limitations of our world in three dimensions as well as the filters our channels apply against stimuli? Nevertheless, their effects appear in diversified forms in our inner world, not as living creatures or in their real shapes.

All religions and schools unanimously believe that the afterworld exists within the heart of this world and many creatures we see in the universe are not real. According to the above illustrations, do we acknowledge these matters?

For distinguishing distance or for giving depth to an image, the brain uses lens alterations and definitions of relationships between lines, angles, and highlights; it implies that for seeing closer objects, the eye lens must have more convexity, and for far objects, the contrary. Thus, our brain creates dimensions in our inner world regarding convexity, so relationships between lines makes us distinguish distance. Thus, according to the fact that dimension is product of a mental definition, it can vary. Look at picture 3. When you stare at this image, you will see the illusion of motion in it, whereas no movement exists and observed motion is product of perception's hallucination due to highlights and relationships between lines.

In fact, we are somehow aware of our mental definitions and perception errors, and we use the same rules to deceive ourselves. Imagine four cameras are to record movement of a single blade fan with different speeds. Camera A only takes one picture at point S from a 360-degree rotation of the blade. Camera B takes two pictures from rotation of the blade at points F and J, and camera C takes four at F, J, G, and N.

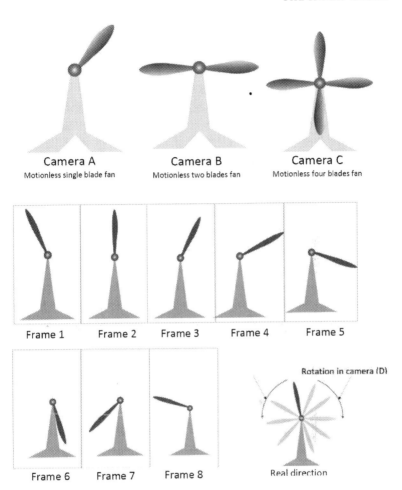

Camera A
Motionless single blade fan

Camera B
Motionless two blades fan

Camera C
Motionless four blades fan

Frame 1   Frame 2   Frame 3   Frame 4   Frame 5

Frame 6   Frame 7   Frame 8   Real direction

Rotation in camera (D)

The fourth camera (D), according to the picture below, takes images each time a little bit sooner than the previous location.

When we look to recorded movies produced by four cameras, we understand the importance of knowing the image-transfer device (the eyes) before any prejudgment about any occurrence. The first camera only exhibits a single blade fan, which seems motionless. The second one shows a fan with two constant blades. The third camera represents a static fan with four blades without any motion. Lastly, the fourth camera, which took each frame a little bit sooner than the previous frame, exhibits a fan that rotates opposite to real direction of the fan and shows a diversified event.

Our eyes, like the above example, takes pictures from external events in the form of frames; and our brain, by attaching these images, shows a movie that is completely different from reality.

If we do not consider the performance method of an image-transfer device, our expression about a unique occurrence could be so different from reality that not only we can not distinguish the direction of the event occurrence, but also we cannot define the number of points and occurrences.

Do speed, direction, number, shape, and manner of events in our inner world conform to reality? One electron, one proton, one atom, one planet—each one is an occurrence in our inner world that has come into view in our perception like this. Does the number of perceived points conform to reality?

Our misconception spawns from the point that we look to ourselves as a perfect and unimpaired observer and forget the fact that our body is somehow a machine which studies universe events via imperfect outputs of senses. This misconception intensifies when senses confirm each other, and it causes us to stay unaware of what truly happens.

In fact, the continuation of our world is due to the imperfectness of our sense channels and stays on until they work in this way. If one day these senses become perfect, our world would collapse and it would leave no trace. Our inner world comes into view in a space with three-dimensional background that causes many perceptional illusions. Nevertheless, this three-dimensional space, contrary to our imagination, is not level and smooth.

SPACE-TIME CURVATURE

In 1919, Einstein, by presenting his general relativity theory in which he used complicated mathematical equations, mentioned that gravity is a geometrical effect of mass on its surrounding space. According to the general relativity theory, the world is not interpretable regarding Newton's rules. He said three dimensions of space are not time-dependent. Moreover, time is a parameter that must be considered in these calculations. He implied that these are interwoven with each other and he called it space-time. Actually, it seems like an invisible structure actually exists. He also proved that space cannot be absolute but it is relative. This space-time continuum can be curved or may be fluctuated. You can only find it smooth in case nothing exists on it.

Wherever a massive object exists, the gravity will be too, and wherever gravity exists, this space-time texture becomes curved. The space curvature determines the way the masses move and travel around this curved space-time continuum.

To explain this fact, he assumed a smooth textile as structure of space-time. Then he put a heavy thing on it (assumed it as the sun) and observed a cavity created in the textile. He said that this curved space-time establishes gravity. The deeper the cavity is, the stronger the gravity would be. Finally, some masses exist in the universe that extend this curvature to its ultimate point and these masses are cosmic black holes.

For a simpler explanation of gravity, we can use this example:

Four people take four corners of a blanket and drag it in order to make it smooth.

The blanket plays the role of space. Now we put an orange on the blanket. It is apparent that the orange will rest in the center. If we put a basketball instead of an orange, more curvature will result due to heavier mass. This curvature on the blanket's (space) surface creates gravity.

If we place the orange on the blanket's edge, it will move toward the basketball. The greater the curvature is, the faster the orange's movement toward the central mass would be.

A black hole is contradictory to cosmic mass. A dark star, an invisible thing, a cage of light—anything that arrives at its boundary will not return. We call it the event horizon—a sphere that swallows anything that enters it for all eternity, a place in which no escape is possible as no solid surface exists on it. Anything, even light, will be swallowed and only a deep maelstrom of gravity remains. These masses are cruel and hunt anything that comes toward them. There is no information available about its center called a singular point. However, we know that a horrible gravity is ruling there. The face of these masses is always hidden and uncovered.

Their singularity point is a point that an extreme gravity is concentrated on. All masses and electromagnetic waves as well as energies that fall into black hole will be compressed into a very small point, and this cause an endless gravity. Black holes swallow star gases greedily. The space is chaotic because of theses masses, and they also compress time and it goes on until the time stops.

The light cannot pass over the event horizon, so scientists assume it as the edge of the universe. It is called the event horizon since all happenings beyond it are hidden from us and we only observe things at the boundary of event horizon. In some black holes, the radius of the event horizon may be only a few kilometers. Anytime a star stabilizes in a binary (double) orbit with a black hole, occasionally it throws some gases toward the black hole and the black hole grabs them via the singular point.

As discussed before, singularity is a point in which density is infinite. In fact, its mass is infinite and its volume is very small. Although a black hole is so powerful that it can pull in all masses concerning dust and gases like a vacuum cleaner, it does not have the ability to hunt.

This is something contradictory to our beliefs. Let us put it in this way: If we put a black hole with the mass of the sun in the center of the solar system, it will not be able to attract planet earth; of course, you can exit the earth and observe interesting events. After getting close to event horizon, you will be elongated. Thus, you can see your feet some kilometers away—of course, if you could stand this force and not shatter. After entering the event horizon, you will decompose into elementary particles, and you will disappear behind the cover of darkness.

The most famous satellites of the Milky Way are two galaxies named the small and big Magellanic Clouds. They create a mysterious curvature in the galactic disk via undergoing actions and reactions with spectral dark matter. It has amazed scientists for a half-century. All these vibrations are composed of almost three notes or three states.

This curvature is seen clearly in a tiny disk of hydrogen gas, which has expanded throughout the whole galaxy. The diameter of the Milky Way is two hundred thousand light-years and the curvature exists throughout it. Scientists noticed that this atomic layer looks like a vibrating drum. Moreover, all these vibrations consist of three notes or states.

Many years before, astronomers denied the probable effect of Magellanic Clouds on galactic curvature since the mass of these two consists of only 2 percent of the disk and the revolution period of these clouds is 5.1 milliard light-years around the galaxy. Thus, it was supposed that these masses are too weak to affect such a large disk, which is two hundred milliard times bigger than the sun.

However, considering dark matter, scientists have tried to explain this subject. Although dark matter is invisible, it is twenty times heavier than all visible matter in the Milky Way. Motion of clouds between dark matter creates a tail that increases the gravitational effect of clouds upon the disk. When scientists compute the dark matter in their simulated model, the Magellanic Clouds create a curvature during their revolution around the Milky Way, which is seen all over the Milky Way.

Actions and reactions of Magellanic Clouds with galactic dark matter, which create a mysterious curvature in hydrogen layers, is the reminder of the paradox, which led to discovery of dark matter thirty-five years ago since astronomers are able to measure the speed of stars and gases located out of galaxy regions by using complicated telescopes. By utilizing these telescopes and measuring the number and mass of stars in the Milky Way, they found out that stars are moving faster than expected.

Suggesting the theory that 80 percent of galaxy mass is dark—that is why it cannot be seen—the astronomers could find a connection between these speeds to the known theories of physics and adopt them. This theory from an astronomical point of view was blasphemous in its time.

The universe is composed of 23 percent unknown dark matter; 4 percent defined mass and energy which is seen as stars, galaxies, and energies between them besides 73 percent dark and undefined energy that I call concealed energy, discovered by NASA in February 2003. This means that we observe only 4 percent of the known universe. The rest of the universe has hidden itself behind a cover of secrets (96 percent).

Although scientists have not discovered the real nature of dark matter, the astronomers would compute it in their dynamic simulation of the cosmos to explain the effect of galaxy curvature upon light of background galaxies, along with the evolution of the galaxy's cluster in the early universe.

If 4 percent of the universe's matter and energy caused such intricacies—from living creatures to inanimate masses and matter—is it impossible for the remaining 96 percent to establish a more diverse subsistence? All living and nonliving creatures are in the territory of this 4 percent. Due to the imperfection of our perceptional channels and devices, we cannot perceive many other beings around us! Do the other worlds with different structures and different rules not coexist?

In fact, the coordinate system we know is composed of three straight lines that have intersected each other at zero point. However, the truth is that the three-dimensional coordinate lines can be straight in space when there is no material point in space.

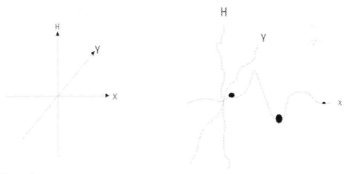

Coordinate axes   Bended coordinate axes

Substance, no matter in microscopic or macroscopic form, bends space; in fact, the special curvatures cause the space coordinate axes to bend. Thus, space is similar to a desert with hills and valleys, of which each particle or material is located at the bottom so each particle of matter is aloof as it separated by a hill from others.

However, none of these particles realize these curves, highs, and hills, since light moves parallel to space over this curved surface. Therefore, each observer will see the object exactly in the direction of light and as far as light travels. Look at the picture below:

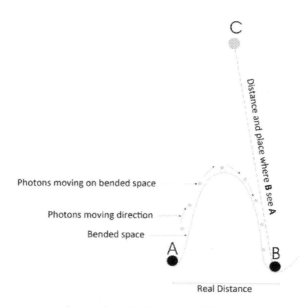

Observer A is located at the bottom of the space curvature and observer B is exactly on the opposite side. The radiated light of observer A moves toward B by slipping on space's curved surface, falling down the hill until A reaches B. Observer B will see the observer A exactly in the direction of light movement in the form of a straight line in point C as long as the hill's length. In other words, none of observers are able to distinguish real places and distances of beings and objects around them. In this state, if observer B wants to move toward observer A, he must begin to move toward C on the surface of space.

As soon as the observer begins to go up the hill, the direction of light toward point A will deviate, and it creates an illusion that the object is located on the straight line and is getting close to point A on a smooth surface.

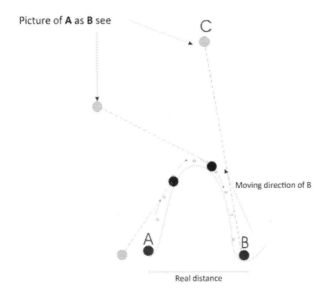

Picture of **A** as **B** see

C

Moving direction of B

A B

Real distance

This means observer B will never realize that he passes through a spatial hill. When you embark on a ship, you imagine that the ocean is the plane and you travel on a surface while the ocean is not level.

Indeed, it is curved like a spatial curvature, but you never realize it!

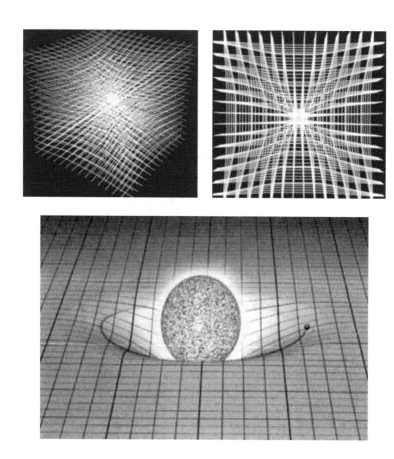

However, even Einstein's theory and spatial curvatures are nothing but rules that dominate our inner world; they are established via creating space and dimensions by tactile and optic senses. If we did not have one of these channels, space and dimension would be meaningless for us or their meanings are not like what we know now, to say the least. Thus, Einstein's relativity theory would not be established.

Movement and distance are parameters that find their meaning via the tactile sense. In other words, the optic channel sees far objects smaller. When we move toward them, the more we get closer and the bigger they would be. In this state, the optic sense only observes that things are getting bigger or smaller; nevertheless, olfaction changes the meaning of the enlargement and shortening into "movement," which itself creates the illusion of distance, space, location, and dimension. In other words, tactility not only makes us perceive the boundary of a body, but also gives meaning to movement, dimension, and space.

Omission of tactility not only eliminates our perception of movement, space, and dimension, but also removes our ability to separate our body from other things—to the extent that we would not consider ourselves disconnected from the environment around us so we would perceive all things due to our inner world as part of ourselves, and we have no perception of volume, shape, distance, and depth. In other words, we will conceive all components of our inner world completely as part of ourselves, but you have no impression of things as you have now.

As mentioned before, the information received from the eyes, which relates us to the real world, is distorted and filtered to the extent that there is practically no similarity between our inner world and real world; nevertheless, we take our inner world seriously to the extent that we do not believe the fact that our considered world is the only world we have built for ourselves at all.

Our mind makes colors. Solidity and the apparent shape of things are the fruits of the imperfection of our sense channels. Locality, place, and distance of things are not real. What we see is a partial trivial thing due to three-dimensional sizes.

If we delete these parameters originated by our mind, what would be left of things?

DO YOU KNOW WHERE
YOUR EYES ARE?

Do not hurry to reply, since they are not located where you think! If you look to the most faraway point in your sensible horizon, your eyes are exactly behind it. Suppose that you seat in a room and your last sensible horizon is the opposite wall, your eyes are behind the image of the wall you see! It may surprise you, but this is reality. Pay attention to this example:

Some friends are sitting in a room. We put someone in a deep hypnotic sleep, and it is 2:30 am and the weather is cloudy; the clouds cover the moon and a mysterious silence dominates the room. The voice of hypnotizer breaks the silence and brings the subject, who is a thirty-year-old man, to a deep sleep. Then he suggests, "You are a six-year-old girl with long hair and blue eyes . . ." The suggestion continues, and the hypnotizer suggests a world which does not exist out of his mind, then continues, "Your twenty-five-year-old mother with golden hair is sitting in front of the window, watching the sunrise. Your father, who has gone out to buy milk, opens the house's wooden door and enters the room, groaning from backache . . ."

The hypnotizer, with his considerable skill, suggests an image of an unreal town, home, friends, neighbors, and all the necessities of his story. Thus, the subject will see himself in a new world with new standards and shapes. Then step-by-step, the hypnotizer suggests all the stages of life gradually until he reaches the age of 18. You must consider that suggestion is practiced with such calmness and skillfulness that the subject even has memories of the past.

He actually sees the suggested story as realistically as what the real world seems to us. At this time, if you ask him where your eyes are, he will point out to the eyes of the girl who is in his dream. If you tell him that his eyes are out there behind those images, he will react the way you did when you were being asked where your eyes are. He observes a virtual world that coexists in his mind.

The location of image formation and perception is in hindbrain, and we observe an image that our brain creates. Like a closed-circuit camera attached to a TV, you watch an image produced by a camera which is placed behind the image.

In other words, we perceive an image that is formed in our brain. Since the brain is imprisoned in the skull, we are observers of insubstantial images of the world within our skull—a world, which, in turn, is made up of objects and beings that are virtual images arising from fluctuations and tiny movements of small particles in a huge space, so what we see is a virtual image of an insubstantial image.

The truth of objects is beyond the world we see, and this world is only an image in our skull. Thus, the real place of the eyes is in the middle point of an image we perceive (inner world) and real world.

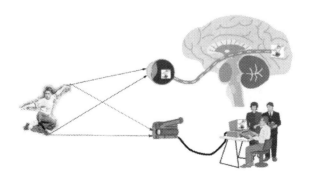

What makes us go wrong even more is an image we built up in our mind while we feel our sensorial perception conform to this image. In fact, we perceive images of our organs—that exist behind this picture—along with other feelings processed in the brain concurrently. So we question ourselves: If it is only an image, how can we touch it? Moreover, how does tactility exactly coincide with it?

All of us know that feelings form in the brain. It means that when someone touches your hand, you feel it in your brain. Do you ever ask yourself if touching occurs in the brain, why do we feel it in our hands? The answer is simple.

Because what we see as the hand that perceives tactility is not the hand itself, but an image of the hand in our brain. In addition, the tactile sense, which is perceived in brain too, is adapted with this image. It means that our real hands are below this image within a few degrees and we look like someone who lives inside his brain. What we call "self" is only a picture of our very "self."

SLEEP AND DREAM

Sleep Physiology

Findings show that transecting the brain stem at the midpoint of brain's cortex causes people to never go to sleep. In other words, it seems there are some centers located below the brain stem which causes sleeping via inhibiting other parts of the brain. Scientists call it the active theory of sleep.

Stimulation of several areas of the brain such as raphe nuclei and rostral part of hypothalamus, mainly in the suprachiasmal area, can produce sleep with characteristics near those of natural sleep. The observations show that neurons of raphe nuclei are serotonergic. In other words, in neural terminals of these neurons, they secrete the neurohormone serotonin, which is associated with inducing sleep.

If we inject a serotonin receptor blocker (such as reserpine) into a laboratory animal, we observe that the animal cannot sleep for several days.

Therefore, we come to conclusion that whenever the sleep centers are not activated, the mesencephalic and upper pontine reticular activating nuclei activate the cerebral cortex and the peripheral nervous system by their spontaneous activation. Moreover, both of them send numerous positive feedback signals back to the same reticular activating nuclei to activate them more.

Therefore, once wakefulness begins, it has a natural tendency to sustain itself because of all these positive feedback signals. Then after the brain remains activated for many hours, even the neurons themselves in the activation system presumably become fatigued. Consequently, the positive feedback cycle between the mesencephalic reticular nuclei and cerebral cortex fades, and the sleep-promoting effects of the sleep centers take over, leading to rapid transition from wakefulness back to sleep.

The time a creature spends for sleeping is of great importance, to the extent that if one, for instance, sleeps less than four hours or more than eight hours, he will be subject to premature death. Sleep has two main physiological effects on nervous system and other functional systems of body: (1) to restore natural balances among the neuronal centers and (2) to reinforce and refresh the body.

It seems that the first one is more important since one who has a transected spinal cord in the neck will not show any physiological effects as far as the sleep-wakefulness cycle is concerned. The lack of a balance between sleep and wakefulness shows no harmful effects on the parts of body under the level of transection.

Prolonged wakefulness is often associated with progressive malfunction of the thought process so that it sometimes causes abnormal behavioral activity in the nervous system. All of us are familiar with increased sluggishness of thought after a prolonged forced wakefulness. Moreover, one can intensively become irritable or even face mental disorders or psychoses. It is hard to keep an ordinary person awake for a long time. Some researchers have done different experiments to pursue the effects of long wakefulness.

It has been proven that after several days of wakefulness, something such as the power of a punch does not change, so muscular actions are not affected. One can still do complicated calculations; hence, the brain's conscious activities are not affected, so one can still press a button rapidly as soon as he sees a flash of light. However, the reaction time apparently becomes longer. What a sleepless person cannot sustain is concentration.

They make too many mistakes, and in order to correct their mistakes, they have to regress repeatedly. After longer periods of wakefulness, these faux pas will develop to the extent that one begins to see things that do not exist; he dreams with opened eyes. This means that the part of the brain in charge of building our inner dreams becomes deranged due to wakefulness and loses its regularity in building inner dreams (the inner world). Routine images of our inner world lose their ordinary stability.

Beings' bodies look like a sack of chemical matters in which few outlets (five senses) have been arranged in order to exchange stimuli and chemical elements with the surrounding environment. Sleep is a state in which beings regulate or stop the exchange of these stimuli by closing some of these outlets. In this state, beings become the observer of their inner occurrences; it means that, in wakefulness, stimuli excite chemical materials via available outlets inside chemical sack of materials (sensorial organs of a creature's body) and create a beautiful, charming world in one's brain. In addition, during sleep, inner stimulations arising from daily activities go on.

In both sleep and wakefulness, creatures are the observers of their inner world. However, in wakefulness, external stimuli take control of building their dreams; during sleep, the remaining impressions of external stimuli besides some other external stimuli—which can pass in spite of closed outlets—penetrate beings and control their dreams and their inner world.

Sleeping is natural in bigger animals and many of them spend one third of their lifetime in this state. During sleep, the secretion of saliva, urea, and gastric juice decrease rapidly; the flow of air into the lungs is reduced; heart rate slows down; and as consciousness diminishes, brain waves transform.

As we gradually fall asleep, alpha waves, which occur at frequencies between eight and fourteen cycles per second, fade; and they move toward long waves of delta with a frequency of one to three cycles per second, which is the sign of deep sleep. Usually, rapid short spindle-shaped bursts of alpha waves occur periodically. Brain waves undergo a significant variation in wakefulness and sleep states; regarding the type of brain wave, you can distinguish the depth of sleep and wakefulness.

Some important known waves are as follows:

1. Gamma waves (26-100 Hz): produced during complicated mental activities, perception, problem solving, anxiety, and panic

2. Beta waves (greater than 12 Hz, usually 20 Hz): appear during wakefulness, disturbed thoughts, active thinking, concentration, and reasoning. Caffeine consumption causes beta waves to appear.

3. Alpha waves (8-12 Hz): appears during relaxation, telepathy, meditation, learning, and daydreaming. It is usually produced by closed eyes and decreases by sleepiness.

4. Theta waves (4-8 Hz): appears before sleep, during sleepiness, short naps, dreaming, deep meditation, hypnotism, trance, praise and worship, spiritual insight, creativity, memorizing, learning, and vivid dreaming. These waves make the information of the subconscious mind available.

5. Delta waves (4 Hz or less): occurs in very deep and less visionary sleep. We can gain access to the subconscious mind via delta waves.

Invertebrates easily become motionless and inactive during sleep, except octopus and cuttlefish. However, in most warm-blooded animals, sleeping is an active process. Sleep is an instinctive pattern since it developed along with an intuitive tendency and special early behavior such as finding a place or moving toward a definite location. By getting dark, some fishes like *Cyprinus carpio* lay flat on the lake bed, and *Mola mola*, the big golden fish, floats on the sea surface sidelong like a huge disk. It seems that these fishes are asleep, and even if you come close silently, you can catch them.

In the case of birds, it is clear that they sleep; during sleep, most of them close their eyes and put their head beneath their wings. Birds that sleep on the tiny branches cannot rest perfectly, and those who sleep on the water's surface often paddle with one leg in order to stay away from the bank and hunters.

Aquatic mammalians must do similar actions, so they come to water's surface occasionally in order to breathe. Dolphins sleep by taking turns keeping one of their eyes open. Cows and many other ruminants sleep while their eyes are wide open; they continue chewing and keep their head up because their digestive system is dependent on gravity. Even animals like elephants and giraffes—that are supposed to be sleepless—in fact, sleep and often lay flat on the floor for sleeping.

All these patterns[5] can be created artificially via electrical stimulation of definite parts of brain. In one experiment, a shock that was given to the upper part of a cat's brain infused (suggested) it to groom itself, circle, and lie down to sleep.

However, more evidence shows that there are some regions in our brain that regulate so-called wakefulness; when these regions cannot be stimulated, we feel sleepy. The region, which is in charge of keeping us awake, is a reticular formation region, which is a kind of senior control in the bottom region of brain for keeping the whole central nervous system activated.

Anesthetic drugs stop this region and bring about sleep until their effects remain, but any mechanical interference in the reticular system stops wakefulness completely and causes long-term coma and death. Consciousness disappears during sleep. However, it may not return upon awakening.

Animals, with their cerebral cortex taken off completely, could still sleep, wake up, move around, eat, and evacuate. However, without this vital gray matter, they could never learn anything or show any sign of real consciousness.

Human psychosis not only affects his dreams but also influences his physical state during sleep. As an example: People who gather their hands and feet together in a bent position have a bashful and sensitive personality. Those who sleep on their back and put their

---

5   Brain waves can be produced artificially by radiation or with voice or electrical stimulation.

hands beside their body are introverted and calm. People that sleep on one side of their body have a sociable and easy personality, and finally, those who sleep on their bellies and put their hands under their heads are rude and fearless.

DREAM OR REALITY

What is a dream, and what is the difference between a dream and reality? What we see as the world and call reality is nothing more than a dream! What is the difference between wakefulness and reality? Are our dreams not another aspect of reality and the world?

When you apparently watch the environment around you via your eyes, you actually see an image which is formed inside you by illuminated waves; when you perceive heat, cold, sound, taste, smell, etc., you observe an inner world which has been built up via sense channel stimulation by external stimuli. Now if the entrance of these stimuli becomes blocked, part of our inner world will be omitted; of course, this omission occurs with a short delay. Since the remaining effects of external stimuli will not fade immediately due to channel blockage, we build up a world within ourselves due to this delay, which is a so-called somatic dream.

Naturally, there are three stages of sleep: somatic (bodily), sensual, and spiritual. Somatic sleep occurs early in the night and in the initial hours of sleep. To become calm and motionless, a creature's body begins to calm down gradually until its excitation due to external stimuli and daily activities stops completely, like a fan which continues rotating after being turned off and slowly becomes motionless.

In this stage, the continuation of daily (bodily) activities arising from reactions of surrounding stimuli and sense channels will appear as a bodily dream. This stage of sleeping usually lasts for two to two and a half hours. This is exceedingly restful and is associated with a decrease in peripheral vascular tone and many other vegetative functions of the body in a way that blood pressure, respiratory rate, and basal metabolic rate decreases 20-30 percent so that neurons find an opportunity for refreshment. This kind of sleep is also called slow wave sleep since, in this state, the brain waves are very strong and have very low frequency.

After passing the first stage of sleep as the person goes deeper into sleep, he enters into the deeper state, which is called sensual dreaming. In this state, the subconscious mind starts resolving difficulties; it means that it rebuilds obsessions, failed desires, fears, and failures via this stage of sleeping, so he makes up for failures or reaches to his desires in a dream. For instance, if someone hits him and causes him hurt mentally during the day, he might see a battle in his dream in which he is victorious. This stage of sleep relates to memories that have been stored in our body and often relates to memories in which chemical materials and hormones have excited due to an external stimulant but have not cooled down, such as concupiscence, hunger, and inferiority complexes, which activate the defense system.

If a part of our nervous system is being excited by an external stimulant without being satisfied, the body will satisfy it virtually by dreaming.

For example, during a stressful situation, the brain reticular formation (the thinking part of brain) sends an alert signal to hypothalamus (the hypothalamus is the main switch of stress response in the midbrain). Then the hypothalamus excites the sympathetic nervous system and some changes appear in the body. These alerts originate from our descriptions about ourselves and the world around us. For instance, if getting angry by impertinence is one of these descriptions, at a time of insolence, the alerting signals appear and move toward the hypothalamus.

The same mechanism that commenced the stress response can cool it down, meaning that when you are convinced the situation is not dangerous anymore, your brain stops dispatching alerting signals to the brain stem, and in turn, the brain stem avoids sending fearful signals. In addition, three minutes later, the battle response stops, and you will return to normal conditions; if the message of stopping does not appear, it may cause chronic stress and, consequently, it may lead to physical and mental abnormalities.

In fact, this part of dreaming is relevant to past memories. It is also in touch with some parts of the body that have remained activated by stimuli while the continuation of their activation would have harmful effects on the body. So with building up a dream of a virtual world in itself, our body will satisfy these parts of the brain (or body), consume residual materials and hormones of body—which is an act of relieving and resolving difficulties—and categorize them by reviewing past memories. This stage of sleep lasts as long as somatic sleep and its interpretations are also relevant to the past actions or unsatisfied mental and emotional excitation. Somatic and sensual dreaming are also called non-REM[6] dreaming.

We assume the body as a relatively constant and permanent structure. The cells have a short life. Not only they are being worn away by friction on the skin surface and gut layers, but they are also being displaced repeatedly in different organs (even bones). After a long time passes, if we meet a friend, it may seem that nothing has changed significantly while none of his body cells have been left unchanged since our last visit.

Rebuilding and renovation requires a new protein combination, and it is being produced during sleep. It seems that the effect on the body's tissues is more pronounced during somatic and sensual sleep. For instance, athletes spend more hours of the day in somatic sleep after heavy sport activities. Hormones are produced during this time lapse and cell division increases by the time sleeping commences.

---

[6]   REM (rapid eye movement)

Contrary to other tissues of body, brain tissues stop growing after a certain age and mostly engage in repair and maintenance. The main growth of brain is done two months before and one month after birth. In this time, the brain's reticular formation is being built, and the newborn baby not only sleeps two times more than an adult, but also proportionate to this, it spends twice as much for sensual sleep. It seems that while a body is renovated during somatic sleep, more blood flows toward the head and creates more heat in the brain.

Most animals have both sensual and somatic sleep; cats and camels, during their whole lifetime, have sensual sleep. In animals with less intelligence, this kind of sleep is only seen in early ages. Sheep and cows, before being weaned, show signs of both types of sleep when their brain is growing, but sensual sleep vanishes completely later. In species such as raccoons and monkeys that are more creative and conscious in all ages of their lifetime, the strong appearance of sensual sleep—rapid eye movement sleep—exists. It seems that there is a close relationship between this kind of sleep, which interacts deeply with dreaming, and higher levels of self-consciousness.

By making an inquiry into the animal world, a kind of consciousness can be represented. At the lowest level of evolutionary development, living creatures become active or completely inactive in alternative time lapses; but in so many progressive species, especially in mammalian animals, this gap is divided into two completely different kinds of sleep, which are linked to divided physical and mental processes. Now human beings step beyond limits that conduct him to a new kind of intelligence.

Sleep produced by drugs is somatic sleep. People who consume somnific tablets, by passing of time, show signs of a person deprived from sensual sleep.

When these people stop using pills, they face intensive reversion of sensual sleep; it seems they compensate for lost time. Under the influence of narcotic drugs, marijuana, and morphine that cause hallucination and intoxication—and they are also pain killers—some dreams are produced. From a biological point of view, the action of these drugs is very similar to that of strong self-suggestion or hypnotism, which causes the same unconsciousness and separation. Besides three drug types, which simulate the main states of life—wakefulness, sleep and dreams—there is another category of chemical materials, which is called hallucinogenic. These materials cause biological abnormalities in the body's system along with too many disorders.

The human mind, after passing sensual sleep, is quieted down as he enters the last stage of sleep, which is spiritual and always happens early in the morning. It is also called REM sleep. In this stage, the sympathetic system is active and the body loses its muscle tone. Muscle tone is continuous and inactive muscular contraction, which helps the sustainability and stability of body.

By relaxation of the body and omission of inner turbulences, the human mind gives a proper opportunity to channels and hidden senses to perceive tiny intangible stimuli and to see the dream very close to reality, which mostly appears as an awareness of future events. The interpretations of these dreams are related to future events and create a real event in our world. This part of dream is influenced by the subconscious mind and telepathic communication with our surroundings. During this kind of sleep, the brain is more activated and its metabolism may increase up to 20 percent.

In such a way that brain waves become surprisingly similar to those during wakefulness, this is a contradictory phenomenon in that, in spite of vivid activity of the brain, the person is still asleep. Here, for a better understanding of the spiritual dreaming process, we take a brief look into the subconscious mind and telepathy.

Subconscious Mind

Human beings have two kinds of conscience: the conscious and the subconscious mind. The subconscious mind is the part which the human being is unaware of its performance and its working spontaneously. This section is not in humans' direct access, while it influences humans' minds and bodies seriously.

The subconscious mind is a place for recording and saving experiences that even the person himself is unaware of. From early childhood and fetal period up to death, what happens around the human being is being recorded in the subconscious mind.

All sensorial experiences (five senses) whether intentional, which has been done voluntarily with complete awareness, or unintentional, of which one has been only the observer, exist in subconscious mind and play their own role.

The subconscious mind records received information without processing and reasoning. In fact, the subconscious mind, in spite of having unlimited power, looks like a child in that, whatever you say or direct, it saves without thinking, reasoning, and processing; moreover, it provides facilities to accomplish the task. It is similar to a motorcar. When you push on the gas pedal, it begins to move without knowing how and where to go!

However, the conscious mind—regarding its knowledge, information, and its reasoning experiences—analyses received cases. Considering personal beliefs, it decides with diversified received information and directs the subconscious mind for action and implementation, so most of the observing, learning, reasoning, and thinking are done by the conscious mind.

Remembering subtle stimuli by the subconscious mind can be seen easily in a simple experiment in which ten meaningless syllables were shown to subjects. Five syllables out of ten were introduced along with an electric shock in such a way that subjects got used to it, and after that, whenever they saw shocking syllables, they felt electrical reactions in the palm of their hands.

In the next stage, they exhibited the syllables so rapidly that no one could detect them consciously. However, the subconscious mind could distinguish those samples clearly and reacted whenever it encountered one of the influencing syllables. The subconscious mind is active all the time. However, we need such methods to force it to expose its information.

We know that under hypnosis conditions, the subconscious mind can remember unbelievable things, such as the number of office steps in an official meeting or the number of light posts in the streets. In fact, nothing—whether partial and intangible or macroscopic and tangible—is kept out of subconscious mind's view, even if the subconscious mind has not seen that or has not concentrated on it.

When you take a brief look at a book, a magazine, or a newspaper, its details will completely be recorded in your subconscious mind, and it is accessible for the conscious mind only when a person is placed in a state similar to hypnotism, trance, or high inner silence.

The subconscious mind is the same as a computer. It has some series of inputs and outputs and a processing zone. The inputs of the subconscious mind consist of information received by the five senses as well as a human's series of thoughts and intellects that feed the subconscious mind continuously.

Record someone's voice on the street. Then listen to it in a silent place. If you concentrate more precisely, you will notice that his voice would fade proportionately due to surrounding sounds, and you will hear peripheral sounds louder than what you were hearing on the street. Take a photograph of that person on the street, then look at it after a while. You can see details hidden from your sight at that moment. In fact, this experiment shows that during the recording of a voice or the shooting of an image, our brain censors many details of voices and images.

However, it does not imply that the eyes and ears do not transmit details to the brain; on the contrary, all details will be transmitted to the brain, but they will be recorded in the subconscious mind's archive and just a selected part or summary of them will be sent to the conscious mind.

To examine the effect of the subconscious mind on the body and consciousness, Stephen Black, a well-known researcher in this area, suggested directly to some hypnotized people that they would not be able to hear a voice with a frequency of 575 cycles per second. In the next examination, this sound was played loudly and promptly, but no physiological reaction was observed. The subjects were not even able to feel the vibration of a diapason attached to their ankle with that same frequency.

Many times, color-blindness or blindness has been tried in hypnosis; it was observed that the brain did not react normally against the bright light. This is a negative sensorial illusion; you cannot see the existing thing. However, positive sensorial illusion has been suggested too, in which bright colors were observed and then some pictures with supplementary colors appeared.

Other physiological mechanisms are subject to suggestion too. In a deep hypnotism, the knee-tendon reaction, which causes the knee to move upward, can be suppressed. You can slow down and speed up the heart rate or increase the blood flow rate in each organ. You can force nearsighted people to change their eyeball (socket) shape and reform their vision for a short time. In addition, the most amazing thing is that the intensive gastric contraction due to extreme hunger can be suppressed only by the suggestion of eating a perfect meal.

Our body is directed by two major subdivisions of nervous system: the sympathetic and parasympathetic nervous systems. The sympathetic control center is in the upper part of the brain, which is associated with the conscious mind as well. This center governs activities such as talking, running, etc., which go along with thinking, selecting, and decision making. The parasympathetic center is in the lower part of the brain and controls activities such as blood circulation, food digestion, etc.

The activity of this part that is more associated with the subconscious mind is normally out of humans' control. The subconscious mind does not have the ability to make decisions and select; it is only a powerful executive manager.

TELEPATHY

As an experiment shows, if you attach two electrodes to a plant, you will realize that, at the time of killing a rabbit or any other living creature, the plant shows high electrical fluctuations, which is the sign of the plant awareness and panic due to the creature's death. If the torture of one creature influences a plant or causes biochemical actions in it, does it not influence other beings too?

You may have heard of the word *telepathy*. Each thing or event is an occurrence that, in order to keep its permanence, needs to change continuously (second law of occurrence—wave). Therefore, when an event occurs inside of a being or happens in mutual relationship between two beings, some waves are produced that propagate all information due to event quality, whether sensual or perceptional and all other occurrences.

Now if some of these unknown waves, according to humans' description of wave (e.g., light, sound, etc.), penetrate a being via input outlets and produce a similar occurrence, which has happened in the other being so the receiver becomes aware of event (or the feelings and perceptions of another creature), it is called telepathy.

Thousands of events recorded seem to have similar stories as the one mentioned above, which occurred mostly between people with highly emotional relationships. Usually, these observations are associated with becoming aware of a crisis that has happened for a pair (husband and wife, father and mother, mother and child, brother and sister) somewhere, and it had been transmitted to each other right at the same time.

The mental relationship between identical twins is the most powerful and distinctive relationship of this kind; they often become sick at the same time. Even if you separate them from early childhood, they live the same way.

In Russia, many researchers have done studies on telepathy via state-supported projects. A new phase began on April 19, 1996: an actor from Novosibirsk named Karl Nikolayev arranged a telepathic contact with his friend Yuri Kaminski, a biophysics scientist, who was three thousand kilometers away in Moscow.

Both of them were under the inspection of a scientific control board, and in a determined hour, Kaminski received a sealed package, which was selected randomly among some similar boxes. After opening the box, he began to touch the object in it, examined it precisely, and tried so hard to make his friend distinguish the object across the distance.

The object was a metallic spring with seven circles, and Nikolayev in Novosibirsk described it with these words: *round, toothed,* and *coil.* Ten minutes later, when Kaminski concentrated on a wrench with black plastic handle, Nikolayev wrote "long and tiny, metal, plastic, black plastic." The probability of guessing a unique target among all possible things is too small to have been talked about. Therefore, the authorities were impressed very much, so some expenses were devoted rapidly for more research.

Shortly thereafter, Popov appeared. This group was a mission of scientists that were known formally as the Bioinformation Institute of the A. S. Popov All-Union Scientific and Technical Society of Radio Technology and Electrical Communications.

Their first target was to distinguish telepathic action in the brain. For this purpose, in March 1967, this mission brought Kaminski to

Moscow again, put Nikolayev in an insulated room in a laboratory in Leningrad, and connected a series of physiological monitors to him. It took time until he assumed an accepting expression—a state which he explains as "completely calm and relaxed, but conscious and focusing" when he signaled that he was ready for the experiment, his brain producing a steady alpha rhythm.

Nikolayev did not know the exact time of telepathic message dispatch by Kaminski. However, exactly three seconds after getting the message from Moscow center indicating the beginning of transmission, Nikolayev's brain waves changed strongly and the alpha waves stopped. For the first time in the history, a vivid reason was attained for thought-pulse transmission from one mind to another with a distance of 640 kilometers.

In the following experiments, the reported results of brain wave recording showed a similarly large variation in brain curves of both sender and receiver.

"We distinguished this abnormal activity of the brain one to five seconds after the beginning of telepathic transmission. We always recognized the transmission, few seconds before Nikolayev consciously became aware of a telepathic message. Firstly, an overall and undetermined activity exists in frontal and middle part of the brain. If Nikolayev decides to receive this telepathic message consciously, the brain activity becomes distinct rapidly and will be transmitted to rear and internal parts of the brain," Popov reported.

When a picture of something such as a cigarette pocket was received, the part relative to the optic channel would begin to act, and when the message included some sort of noise heard by sender, the activity associated with brain temple area of the receiver, which is usually related to sound, would occur.

There is a certain relationship between telepathy and alpha rhythm. Telepathy certainly happens under distinguished psychological circumstances, and it occurs by means of brain waves—alpha waves—with a frequency between eight to twelve cycles per second. People who get good grades in such experimental exams declare that they assume a special mental expression. One of them explains it as follows: "To concentrate on a point of nowhere, I do not think about anything. I just look at the fixed point and set my mind free as far as possible." Another one calls this telepathic state "concentrated," and another one explains it as "released consciousness and attention."

There are two kinds of attention. The first one is the active type which needs effort. For instance, imagine a dinner party in which a person tries to listen to unwanted and boring advice of a nearby person who talks softly; meanwhile, guests laugh out loud and talk about interesting and amazing things. This kind of attention involves struggling. Another type is a passive state in which a person responds to an exciting sensory effect instinctively. Assume the state of person who wakes up promptly and thinks that something must have disturbed his sleep. He sits, watches, listens, and waits for something that may happen again.

Production of telepathic phenomena is still so rare that it is still assumed unusual. The state of attention without struggling, which exists in successful telepathic sessions, is the remarkable sign of this psychological condition, which goes along with alpha waves.

For production of these waves, which turn on the "alpha phone" lamps, one must attain a passive state. People think that alpha waves are produced until their eyes are closed, and as soon as they open their eyes, they will be stopped spontaneously. You can continue producing waves with completely open eyes with practice in such a way that you can avoid the processes of thinking, analyzing, and calculating. It means to avoid any sensory and bodily activity as long as possible.

This is an explanation for why many mental experiment subjects insist on working in a calm atmosphere and also prefer to work in darkness or in low light, to say the least.

The experiment of Einstein's brain wave recording showed he was keeping his alpha waves approximately continuous even during relatively complicated calculations. However, in this case, this was a part of his routine life, and he did not put too much effort into it. It seems that there is no need for alpha waves to be disconnected via brain activities. Of course, this is only applicable for activities which do not need active attention or do not oppose each other.

Popov's group built an automatic harmonizer machine, which is in fact an "alphaphon," that let Karl Nikolayev know whether he has suitable conditions to receive telepathic messages or not. It seems the coexistence of similar waves in both sender and acceptor is the primary and necessary condition for a successful connection between two people. In addition, Russian researches have shown that the similarity of brain's patterns is not accidental. In one of these experiments, Kaminski was in front of a photography lamp that was turned off and on with diversified frequencies in the alpha range, and this excitation naturally produced similar waves in his brain.

In another building, Nikolayev prepared himself to produce his alpha waves for reception of telepathy. When they both supposedly established the connection, surprisingly, it was discovered that their brain patterns were completely harmonized. Moreover, due to variation of twinkling lamp frequency, Nikolayev's brain waves were changing promptly in order to adapt to the lamp.

Similar results have been achieved by Thomas Jefferson University in Philadelphia. Two ophthalmologists showed that any alteration in brain waves of identical twins, for instance—alpha wave production in one of them—could produce similar alteration in another one from a long distance.

If a strong physical or emotional condition occurs, this kind of mental connection becomes more effective. The Popov association put dual glasses on Kaminski's eyes that could provide different twinkling frequencies for each eye. This double excitation created contradictory patterns in two sides of his brain, so it caused him to vomit immediately. The same patterns appeared in Nikolayev's brain exactly at the same side of his brain, and he became so seasick that the session was discontinued.

Telepathy can be established between animals and plants, humans and animals, or plants and animals, and this is of a great importance since our subconscious mind is able to record and save all these relations completely. Moreover, they are accessible for the conscious mind in special conditions.

Several experiments and observations have been done in diversified countries. Experts tried to discover the mysteries of the plant world. One experiment happened accidentally in 1966 in a New York police office.

One day, Clare Baxter, an expert in lie detector machines, accidentally attached the machine to the leaf of a dracaena plant and watered it. He expected that the plant's water content would cause the galvanometer to show lower resistance in electrical current transmission, but it happened conversely. He decided to burn that leaf, but even before putting his decision into action and sending out his lighter, he saw that the pointer of the machine deviated intensively. In other words, the plant's superficial conductance had increased.

Recorded curves of these variations were very similar to the electroencephalogram of the person who had been under torture. When Baxter burned the leaf, the current intensity was weaker, but when he decided to pretend burning the leaf, he did not see any reaction. It seemed that plant had been aware of his untrue decision.

Through other experiences, Baxter found out that plants feel human impressions and react emotionally before their owner. He also found, in the other experiment, that plants have a kind of memory. The experiment was held by using this method: They closed the eyes of six people and asked them to select folded papers. Something was written on one of papers that had asked the selector to destroy one of the two plants in the room. In this condition, no one could identify who the person was, then some electrodes were placed on both plants, and the six suspected people passed in front of the target plant orderly.

Surprisingly, it was observed that when the one who had the mission to destroy the plant approached the target plant, the machine pointer began to fluctuate. It was assumed that the plant had distinguished him, or it had perceived the matter, which he had been trying to hide through a kind of telepathic connection.

Another experiment was done to determine the mental connections between animals and plants; some lobsters were placed on a metal plate which was vibrated due to lobsters' movement, and then they fell down into a bowl of hot water. In a nearby room, there was a plant attached to the galvanometer, and at the time of the lobsters' death, it drew chaotic and uneven curves that were not similar to preceding curves. It seems that these curves are associated with death perception of some cells by other cells. However, this kind of connection cannot be established via electromagnetic waves since neither a leaden wall nor a Faraday cage is able to cut it, just as when a connection between a plant and its owner is established, distances and barriers are not able to disconnect it.

The Russians have been able to establish conditional reactions in plants as well. A research association from Alma-Ata University in Kazakhstan taught one plant to hate a special dog that had a special mineral in its body. As soon as the dog was near the plant, they exposed the plant to burning, cutting, and electrical shock; after a short period, when this dog approached, the plant would react. Such reaction, which was recorded by galvanometer, was not accomplished with the approach of other dogs.

During recent researches, Italian and German scientists concluded that plants are conscious; they react in dangerous situations, and they even inform other plants and living creatures. When plants feel danger, they display fear and inform other plants via spreading a special smell into the air. Some people believe that plants send alarm signals to other plants to ask for help.

We can see this kind of connection in human beings. However, in a conscious state, human feelings and perceptions remain inaccessible for the subconscious mind due to some poisonous and unnecessary thoughts. However, moment by moment, the subconscious mind records everything and saves it in detail under special conditions, especially in spiritual dreaming, meditation, or mystical trance; it appears as intuition, knowledge, wisdom, awareness of future events, etc.

SPIRITUAL DREAMING

From one point of view, spiritual dreaming can be considered as territory of the subconscious mind. The subconscious mind is not only able to receive weak waves including telepathy, but can also remember external stimuli which has observed details in the form of hearing, seeing, or other feelings during the day while the conscious mind is unaware of them. With the help of new stimuli that it receives from its surroundings, it begins to analyze and rebuild the result of its analysis as dreams.

In fact, our subconscious mind can perceive some stimuli due to our surroundings and compare them with its memories that are to form future events, just as in earthquakes, which deer and rabbits can predict several hours before they happen.

When people are dreaming, they take it as reality and forget their wakeful world completely; as soon as they wake up, by watching their second dream (inner world), they assume that what they have seen as a dream is unreal due to one's incapability to return to that dream scene or make a logical connection between night dreams.

Living beings are living in their mind and in their imaginary world, which exists due to the imperfection of perceptional channels in their lifetime. They perceive the world in two states of sleep and wakefulness. Since they have more choices in wakefulness and can make a more logical connection among events, they assume that their dreams are illusive and try to justify the dream world (spiritual dreams) based on their perceptions as well as their inner world, but they cannot succeed; it is why they do not accept it as truth. The real world does not have anything in common with their perceptional worlds, whether in sleep or wakefulness, unless in partial things. Sleep and wakefulness are both shadows of reality.

Regarding the discussion about sensory perceptions, our wakeful world is nothing but dream—a dream which seems real due to the constancy of its foundations. In fact, we are sensitive to some stimuli of the existing universe and perceive them in wakefulness, whereas we perceive some other subtle stimuli of the universe during sleep.

It looks like changing TV channels; we can watch channel 1 or 2 anytime we want. In fact, two channels coexist simultaneously, but this is the receptor sensitivity which determines which channel to broadcast. However, human beings cannot perceive both worlds (sleep and wakefulness) simultaneously due to the imperfection of perceptional channels, unnecessary concentration on dreams of this material world, and thought confusion.

Actually, we live in two worlds during our material life with some differences; one of them is continuous and longer than the other one, and these two worlds (sleep and wakefulness) form our inner world. Of course, we perceive superior aspects of the time in our dream that is impossible in wakefulness by our material body, unless in special conditions.

While sleeping, subconscious mind perceptions and surrounding receptions, telepathy waves, the conscious mind, environmentally received waves, and also stoppage and alteration of the filtering parts of perception—which builds dimension, space, color, taste and smell, solidity, and generally all rules and forms of the wakeful world—perceive superior forms of the external world in a perfect manner. Therefore, we understand connections among events, things, and beings better. Moreover, our intelligence predicts future events and manifests it as true images and dreams in our perception via analyzing these data during spiritual dreaming.

DOMINATION VIA SPIRITUAL DREAMING

As mentioned previously, all diversified religions describe the perception advancement in understanding of higher aspects of the world as if human beings perceive the world with their incorporeal shapes, which own superior aspects in spiritual dreaming.

In fact, the material body we see is an image of our body's shell and its outer surface, which the optic channel shows us; therefore, all imperfections due to seeing the world and its elements such as color, volume, shape, solidity, and dimension are applicable to our body image too. Thus, no one can say what the human body really looks like.

What we see as ourselves is an imperfect image of our real body, which has been formed in our skull. During sleep, this virtual image collapses and we perceive the other image with different characteristics; the same happens in dying.

Across history, some great masters who were aware of this natural process of sleep decided to use it for reaching knowledge and knowing the existing universe through connecting to the subconscious mind and telepathy waves. They also discovered that, by this method, they are not only able to be aware of future and past events but it is also possible to communicate with creatures such as plants, animals, nonorganic beings, etc. Therefore, they invent some methods in order to attain spiritual dreaming in wakefulness. They knew that, for attaining this level, bodily excitations must reach its minimum value.

In addition, internal dialogue must be completely extinguished; internal dialogue is a kind of talking to oneself by which human beings continuously review the past, present, and future of themselves and others and mistakenly call it thinking, whereas they are so scattered, inconsistent, irrelevant, sickening, and chaotic in a way that you cannot find any logical connection among them. This internal dialogue scatters mental power and decreases cautiousness as well as consumes a considerable amount of body energy, and it distracts the main attention of human beings from environmental stimuli. Sensual excitation, which often originates from human needs and instincts, must be cooled down.

Hence, their methods and trainings are divided into two parts. Firstly, they use methods to extinguish internal dialogue compulsorily by deceiving the mind and conduct the body to its most relaxing possible state. The methods are like closing the eyes and concentrating on a distinguished point by staying conscious and relaxing all body muscles—also by making the environment quiet along with concentrating all senses on one point by staring at it and by using methods such as meditation, TM, trance, deep breathing, self-hypnosis, etc., by which mind and body become relaxed and go deep into a pretend sleep—and hence in wakefulness, the conscious mind passes somatic sleep.

The second part of their training was designed for passing sensual sleep, regarding the fact that sensual sleep originates from mental excitations, which is imposed on humans by the environment or inner instincts. It was somewhat complicated since the rate of domination over it was related to the rate of awareness and knowledge of a human being's mind.

They also perceived the fact that human beings are unable to act only through knowing something. Therefore, they use fear, pleasure, and love to push their followers to follow their instructions regularly since they found out that these three factors are the main motives of humanity.

There is fear of the unknown that makes human beings fanatical. There is greed of gaining more pleasure in the afterworld, which attracts them to recommended religious precepts, and finally, love makes the pain, suffering, and hardness easier and more versatile. Thus, some masters proposed monastic life and staying away from any sensual excitations; so via establishing temples or seeking caves and faraway places, they tried to omit this part of the dream, and finally, they attained good achievements.

These successes consisted of becoming aware of future and past events; knowing properties of plants, animals, elements, and sicknesses; and attaining special abilities that normal people could not reach. Unfortunately, human beings have gone to extremes because of the sanctification of one school of thought and the exaggeration of its followers. Therefore, they turned to some kind of self-torment and to excuse their behavior, and they considered the goal of these acts of self-torment as gaining God's satisfaction. That is how they mislead themselves and others. The school of Jainism is one of hundreds of ideas that unfortunately became involved in such a destiny. A person from a wealthy family established this school in the middle of the sixth century BC.

His parents were the followers of a school that considered poverty as an honorable thing. They respected suicide due to intensified austerity and considered it as privilege and prestige. When he was in his thirties, his parents ended their lives with intentional hunger. This event affected his mind. He turned his back to the world, took off his clothes, and became homeless in West Bengal like the ascetics. He did some works and researches for purification of the soul and for self-knowledge. He struggled thirteen years for this reason. Some people followed him, and after that, they called their leader Mahavira ("the great champion) and due to his remarkable and distinguished beliefs called the school Jain. Mahavira determined a group of single men among his followers, and he gathered a group of nuns as well. He died at the age of seventy-two and had nearly fourteen thousand followers. This school gradually became one of the strongest religions of the history. Nakedness was part of their austerity; also, it was a way to reach absolute truth, and it was the end of all pains.

Their followers must not put on clothes to cover their nakedness. Some followers did obey this rule, and some of them did not pay attention to it. They are divided into two groups, naked and dressed ones. That is why they were struggling with each other. Nowadays, only a few of them obey this rule. Jainism is divided into eighty-four castes. Initial teachings of Jainism included total hunger and nakedness to the extent that if he died, he could reach a high ranking. Suicide through asceticism was a part of this austerity.

Vegetarianism is part of monastic life of Jain school. They believe that such abstemiousness can exterminate wicked roots of materialism from human essence so that he becomes illuminated and does not get involved in the calamity of metempsychosis.

In Taoism, one must form his beliefs based on special mysticism and pantheism; and in order to reach that goal, he must stay away from attaining knowledge and playing with words and reject the pleasure of the material world. He must keep away from reasoning and go deep inside himself by spiritual revelation. He must become indifferent to events and occurrences and must be thoughtless and unaware of anything and anyone. He must enter into a world of trance with dance and music. This is the first step toward the Tao religion.

Some masters recommended staying in society and making body and mind jointly calm along with everyday life since, in spite of some hardships, they found that the result is far greater and gained power is more extraordinary than that of monastic life. Gradually, ancient masters increased their knowledge about the human mind and body by joining the experiences of themselves and others and, consequently, proposed new ways and improved previous methods. Of course, this causes differences among human schools and training methods of each master.

In the following, these schools of thought succeeded in exploring special remedial methods via telepathic communication with plants and animals, including acupuncture, cupping (bleed by cupping), herbal therapy, etc.

By accessing special abilities and connections with other creatures, they acquired more knowledge about human totality, the existing universe, and God that had been forming basics of their philosophy.

Later, self-control and staying away from jealousy, anger, hate, regret, dependence, passion, pride, sadness, worry, stress, self-centeredness self-compassion, etc., became known as continence and killing egocentric desires; moreover, the methods used to reach to these goals became the main essentials of these schools. This caused people to respect these groups and sanctify them since they were able to help people in solving their problems. Besides, because of their self-control, they were reliable, relating to people's properties, lives, and chastity.

Unfortunately, many calamities befell these schools. It includes two main parts: (1) misinterpretations of the school's followers due to their ignorance and (2) some impure people misusing the name and appearance of schoolmasters.

Regarding the fact that the understanding of each person about unique subjects depends on his perceptional memories, ignorance, and unawareness—these, along with the history of humankind, have always caused misinterpretation of great masters' trainings and sentences (whether prophets or schoolmasters). This was especially the case when one school's followers—still not having attained the degree of a perfect master—began to teach or interpret the methods and words of their masters who have died. Moreover, they related their own thoughts and presumptions to that school. The following story shows one type of unintentional distortion.

One day, there was a cat in a temple which was a constant pest to their concentration. Thus, the great master ordered someone to catch the cat at the time of meditation, take it to the end of the garden, and tie it to the tree. This procedure went on for many years and became one of their basics. Many years later, the great master died, and later on, the cat died too. The monks brought the other cat and brought it to the temple in order to tie it up to the tree during meditation to set the rules of meditation. Many years later, one of the foolish followers of the school, who claimed that he is a master, wrote a treatise about tying a cat to the tree during meditation. Later on, an interpretation was written about the treatise, which explained properties of diversified colors of cats and the kind of tree and rope by which it must be tightened!

The other calamity was excessive admiration and courtesy that people considered for founders of these schools. People considered a special position for them to the extent that presumed them as governors of the existing universe who were able to do anything, especially in the afterworld life. So in order to attain respect and comfort and set themselves free from the fears of afterworld, they flattered these masters. Meanwhile, some incompetent people—who were mostly involved in emotional and personal deficiencies and who were greedy for esteem, power, and obedience of their fellow men—misled these schools by untrue exaggeration of their followers.

The appearance of the Brahman religion resulted from the distortion of the Veda religion that was done by formal and informal clergies. The Veda religion, which was the crystallization of humane idea (thought) in India, became meaningless and senseless in the dogmatic system of Hindu clergymen. They took the gnostic spirit of Veda and replaced it with sorcery. That is how they added to the stupidity of Indian people and prepared a business for themselves.

Clergies knew the rules and methods of offering a sacrifice and had the right to do it in person or via their representatives and receive rewards, which were often precious animals or cows.

In order to formalize their authority, they distorted holy textbooks of the Veda religion. In verse 10 of the tenth book of the Rigveda, it is written: "In return for satisfaction of one cow which is given to Brahman clergy, the total universe will be rewarded." They laid the groundwork of their presence in later generations of humane thought in India. In Veda textbooks, an intensified clergyism is seen by which they can explain the transition of the Veda religion to Brahma.

The second group was people that tried to deceive people by misusing the popularity of some masters, imitating their style of clothing and costumes, and circulating superstitions and misinterpretations among people. They caused these schools to branch out via the distortion of great masters' trainings and quotations regarding their impure intentions. Thus, they become deviated.

In time, while discovering the way human beliefs are formed, ancient masters (I mean the real ones, not those who gathered some people for diversified purposes) attained a greater discovery. That was the discovery of a wonderful and endless power in human beings—the subconscious mind. Deep down in each human mind, there is an ocean of intelligence, wisdom, ability, and endless knowledge. All human beings live on a vast stage of endless wealth. They can utilize infinite blessings and powers within themselves; and by using wonderful and magical inner powers, they can gain access to salvation, inward calmness, happiness, good health, wealth, light, beauty, and love, and keep away from indecency, jealousy, disturbance, depression, and generally all mental and physical sicknesses.

The subconscious mind has such a great power that can easily solve all emotional, financial, and health problems. They found out that the subconscious mind is an extraordinary power, an infinite treasure and an endless potency which all humans are benefiting from. Thus, the ability and facilities of each person are unlimited, and no one is superior to the others in this matter.

However, this endless power looks like a double-edged sword. If we use it correctly, we will have a wonderful and happy life, whereas due to people's unawareness toward its unlimited power and by misusing it, most people prepare an unwanted life full of stress, pain, sickness, poverty, and wretchedness.

Ancient masters utilized the disability of the subconscious mind in analyzing and processing data; they recommended to their followers suggestion, deliberation, positive thinking, imagination of favorite things, and especially positive questions through using different forms, such as religious songs and elevated thoughts as well as putting their subconscious mind along with their goals.

Since they saw ordinary people devoid of elevated goals, they designed religious songs, spells, and prayers. They taught their followers, determined subjects, to repeat them daily, especially before sleep and after wakefulness as creating beautiful images of their favorite goals in their mind and questioning themselves via elevated thoughts.

Insistence on good deed and good thought, pure intents, and hopefulness were the fundamentals of these songs. The masters discovered that every time these songs were repeated, they were recorded in the subconscious mind exactly, and due to repeating and archiving, the subconscious mind assumed the repeated songs as favorable, and the matters would be reflected from subconscious mind for action. The subconscious mind, affecting by repetition on and on, changes its beliefs gradually and produces new beliefs parallel to suggested concepts and matters along with putting new beliefs into practice too.

The greater the repetition of messages, signals, and suggestions are, the faster the performance of the subconscious mind would be. Hence, this causes the process of the alteration of beliefs shorter. The subconscious mind does not understand repetition; in other words, it does not assume the repeated subject as a repetitious topic. For instance, if we repeat a sentence one hundred times, it records it one hundred times, and then suppose it appears one hundred times as new signs and messages. That is why they forced their followers to repeat their deed and spells greatly.

By growth and expansion of their ideology, ancient masters found out that human beliefs—that are governors of human behaviors—were formed in all stages of his lifetime. However, constructed beliefs from birth up to five years old are of a vital importance since, during this period, a child is intensively dependent on his mother, father, and relatives without knowing the concept of good and bad or without being able to understand meanings; he receives instructions, orders, punishment, encouragement, and warnings from relatives and records them. Besides, the child records whatever the mother and the other relatives do via hearing, seeing, and touching. In addition, he precisely observes and records events and routine daily matters, customs, formalities, religions, and related ceremonies.

During this time, the child's situation, his vital need for parents and his inability to understand meaning and concepts make it impossible for him to modify and explain matters. Therefore, he assumes all matters and events as completely true and saves them. These recorded tapes exist during his whole life, and he cannot delete them from his mind. These tapes are always ready to play again. This has a powerful domination during his life span.

Thus, orders, alerts, instructions, punishment, encouragements, etc., are recorded in the child's brain that most of which creates negative feelings in a framework of words—*do, do not, never, always, do not forget to*—and also creates absurd and boring corrections of parents. These unhappy feelings, which come one after another and confirm each other, are recorded continuously and are not omissible. Bad and good memories—along with surrounding parameters such as air temperature, existing smells, voices, and scenes at that time—are being saved in memory and create conditional states that whenever one of these parameters is provided, that memory revives.

To understand better the practical role of the subconscious mind through a lifetime, this example would help. Imagine a ten-year-old child who is subjected to torture.

The story finishes and everybody tries to hide that matter. Many years pass by, and apparently, the matter ends well. Everybody forgets that event—even the child himself, being unaware of the fact that the unpleasant experience has been recorded in the subconscious mind. After marriage, a problem with so-called frigidity appears which appears in different forms, such as the lack of sexual pleasure, not reaching orgasm, and too many complicated problems.

Constructed beliefs and presumptions of this period are of a special importance since later beliefs are affected by initial beliefs. Even in many people, their five-year-old thought formation and beliefs remain unchanged and will partially guide them through their whole life fanatically, so some of the ancient masters who believed in correction of total society via establishing temples tried to educate students from early childhood.

They also tried to impose their beliefs on people through contributing in the tribe's involvements and forcing them to accept their training since they knew a child who grows up in such an environment tends to these basics severely and obeys them spontaneously.

Unfortunately, wrong transmission of ancient masters' teachings to future followers happened due to the ignorance of most people, misinterpretation of great masters' quotations, wrong understanding, and fanatical interpretation parallel to personal profits.

From early childhood—influenced by negative speech, deed, and suggestions of relatives, especially our mother and father—we learn that life is hard, rough, and cruel. Life is mortal. You are inefficient. You always make mistakes. You must be ashamed. You must grieve for what you do not have or what you have lost. You must only care about what people think about you and consequently try to be what they admire and many such suggestions. Unfortunately, many of these negative beliefs remain in people for their life span.

Regarding what was mentioned above, beliefs and presumptions of human beings are built up from early childhood without the person's interference. Early beliefs affect later ones. Furthermore, many human characteristics and their ways of thinking are influenced by the dominant culture of society, suggestions, and surrounding models (family and society) in such a way that most of the time, resistance against them, even in higher ages, is very difficult.

Ancient masters found out that without caring about questions such as where we have come from, how our childhood has elapsed, what difficulties we have had, and how society's beliefs influenced (positively or negatively) our beliefs, we can produce a successful, calm, healthy, attractive, wise, powerful, positive, and joyful humans out of ourselves. Moreover, we are capable of being a novel human with different personality. Thus, they engaged in designing and training methods which could help human beings reach these goals.

They discovered that if we do not learn how to use and control the unique potency of our subconscious, we would certainly not utilize its benefits. Besides, misusing it will cause unpleasant events and irreparable damage.

One of the main functions of the subconscious mind is to build up positive or negative beliefs in human beings. In other words, the subconscious mind is a factory to construct beliefs. Our beliefs and presumptions are the most important elements of the body and mind since

1. Overall appearance, sicknesses, personality, intelligence and memory, body abilities and disabilities, tolerance and consistency, reactions and intentions, friendships and enmities, choices, fears and hopes, worries and stresses, sorrows and grieves, desires and goals, and behaviors and deeds are influenced directly by our feelings, beliefs, thoughts, and knowledge. (It has been explained in volume 2, Matter and Intelligence, in detail.)

2. Our thoughts arise from faith, beliefs, and presumptions that have been fixed by the lapse of time, and this occurs in our subconscious mind.

On the other hand, negative thoughts intensify disabilities, inadequacies, and inferiority complexes; and many other negative characteristics reduce self-confidence intensively. As meeting a problem, it tells us that you cannot, you are not capable, and you will lose. Consequently, it works against our benefit; thus, it practically prevents our progress. For instance, assume that a wooden board 25 cm in width is placed at a 0.5-m altitude and you will be asked to pass the board. Your conscious mind and subconscious mind tell you unanimously that you can pass it easily.

Now if they put that same piece at a four-meter altitude and ask you to pass it, you may tell yourself, "I have passed it before and I can pass it again." Here, the subconscious mind says that this is dangerous and may cause you to fall and hurt, so when you first step onto the board, your legs begin to shiver, your head staggers, and you will be unable to continue moving.

Faith was one of the main basics that ancient masters discovered for its value, so they utilized it for their trainings. In fact, they found out that there are three kinds of beliefs: verbal belief, heart belief (faith), and certain belief.

Verbal belief is the knowledge of the conscious mind, which is based on science, apprehensions, and hearing. These beliefs are fluent with words without having any practical value. In fact, one's knowledge is not apparent in his actions (as many religious people claim). This means that a person's subconscious mind—or even conscious mind—does not believe it completely, and he is still in doubt, like the story of the board mentioned before.

Beliefs of this type—because of being superficial—have a slight influence on a human being's life and physics. These are mostly claims that we utter for different reasons.

Heart belief: This is a belief that has been accepted by the subconscious mind. This belief is of a special importance in life and material body since it causes a human to pass an acrobat rope safely or improve one's battle with blood cancer.

Deep beliefs determine our appearance, morality, behavior, courtesy, actions, decision making, illness, taste, and quality of our life. In fact, whenever there is a contradiction between the conscious mind (verbal beliefs) and the subconscious mind (deep beliefs), the subconscious mind would win.

Thus, actions, behaviors, deeds, and our daily life show our deep beliefs. In fact, it is not important how one introduces himself and his beliefs; the decisive matter is his actions since his deep beliefs, more than appearing in his words, are revealed in his actions.

It resembles the difference between you and a ropewalker that walks easily on the rope. This is because his (subconscious) mind regards that walking on the rope is possible at higher altitudes, whereas yours considers it impossible. Another is that your subconscious mind contrasts your conscious mind. Ropewalker's conscious mind says, "I can do it for sure," and his subconscious mind acknowledges it; but in your case, your conscious mind says, "I can," while your subconscious mind does not believe it. Self-confidence, an inferiority complex, and a human being's mental health are directly associated with this part of our beliefs.

Therefore, great masters, after becoming aware of the unique power of the subconscious, found out that in order to create great and everlasting effects as well as manifest hidden powerful potency within human beings, they must excite deep beliefs of people due to their powers, existing universe, and God, so that they could lead people to gain their totalities and save them.

We are powerful creatures! We are the absolute rulers of the universe, but we have used our power to ruin ourselves due to lack of self-reliance, self-confidence, disagreement between conscious and subconscious mind, lack of a healthy life, and following our desires.

Unity between the conscious and the subconscious mind can create a miracle. It can heal an incurable person or make a healthy person completely sick. It can turn a friend into enemy, and conversely, turn an enemy into a friend or make an impossible thing possible and vice versa.

Finally, let us talk about certain belief. When there is a complete agreement between conscious and subconscious mind apprehensions—provided that this is confirmed by life events and occurrences along with extinguishing inner turbulences and deleting diversified thoughts and internal dialogue—one knowledge becomes more evident in comparison to the other beliefs. It overshadows the other thoughts, intentions, corporal, and emotional desires, choices, and targets. In fact, certainty appears in terms of deletion of inner turbulences and internal dialogues as well as deep concentration on one or more deep beliefs. In other words, certain belief is a belief that has taken control of other deep beliefs via inner silence in order to extinguish them.

When a human being reaches certainty, he will put it in practice. This performance is called a wonder or miracle. In diversified religions, this has always been referred to this a human being's potential. In the Quran, God says, "I am the God who command things to be, then they are; obey me and avoid vice in order to acquire God's Power."

Another master tells this via his trainings: "When a warrior seeks something with his totality, his request appears as God command then it will be accomplished."

A laser is built of parallel light rays in this order: two heads of a ruby beam are coated with silver in a way that it makes a mirror on one side and a half-mirror on its other side. Then a neon lamp is turned around it. (Look at the picture below.)

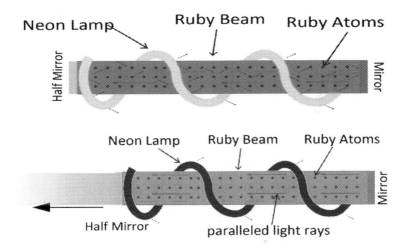

When the lamp lights up, light rays are dispatched to the ruby and collide ruby atoms. This collision causes reflection of rays from atoms and subsequently from mirrors of both sides. As time passes, the rays that are being reflected between two mirrors exceed and form a bigger beam of parallel rays. When these parallel rays become powerful enough, they exit from the half-mirror side of the ruby, and then a laser is produced.

Human thoughts are exactly as scattered light rays that are drawn to everything. These thoughts are the main part of our being that are able to control our life. Everyone can have more than sixty thousand thoughts every day; it implies that mental power is divided into thousands of absurd and poisoned thoughts. It causes our perception to be giddy and vague and subsequently avoids manifestation of the real power of our thoughts. In fact, the amount of awareness and attention you have in ordinary life is one-thousandth of your real consciousness, but you never realize it since you have gotten used to it and so have other people.

When you go shopping for clothes and choose a shirt among different shirts, you may imagine that your mind is concentrated on a few fixed shirts while the reality is something else. In fact, you are the observer of the final result of reviewing a thousand memories from early childhood up to now. Your mind even reviews memories of the subconscious mind of which you are not aware. Now if a human being could make his thoughts parallel and omit his absurd and meaningless thoughts, and also if he could extinguish his internal dialogue and concentrate on a unified subject, he would act as a laser beam in a way that the power of mind's parallel thoughts would be fired in one direction, and consequently, a miracle would happen.

We continuously choose negative or positive thoughts—consciously or unconsciously, intentionally or unintentionally. We even sometimes repeat them obstinately. Negative feelings are being placed in our thoughts unintentionally in the form of doubts, questions, comparisons, judgments, anger, jealousy, selfishness, hopefulness, and hopelessness. However, positive thoughts must be injected into our subconscious via suggestion. Therefore, when positive or negative thoughts are being repeated in our mind, regarding the connection between body and mind, their positive (safe) or negative (unsafe) influences on our body continue permanently.

When we have negative thoughts in our mind, intentional or unintentional, we repeat them thousands of times every day. Consequently,

1. Negative thoughts gain more power and become more stabilized.
2. Negative thoughts allocate more space in the mind, so day after day, we become weaker in controlling them and finally get sicker and sicker.
3. Finally, they take a total part of thought production under control and make our thoughts negative in nature, and it causes our body to form based on our thoughts in such a way

that it obviously shows our negativity to others' subconscious mind. Besides, we put a negative filter on our perceptive channels that interprets everything in the worst way, so we do the best to torture ourselves as well as others.

4. Dispatched signals to our surroundings cause negative reactions come toward us as well as keep positive things away.

Ancient masters found out that gathering enough energy is essential for changing our thoughts into deep beliefs. The energy is attained via taking total control of feelings, internal fluctuation, internal dialogue, and negative feelings. Since each thought and feeling appears as a sign and chemical code in brain, the domination over them leads us to take control of biological activities of body; therefore, this is the first step toward accessing power and transcendence.

Inner silence and concentration just controls the conscious aspect of our body, so to harness our unconscious level more deeply, feelings such as anger, passion, fear, stress, worry, desperation, jealousy, laziness, selfishness, self-importance, hypocrisy, inferiority, etc., must be controlled completely. Therefore, they understood that the only way to attain and store energy is to take control over these feelings so that the unique power of the subconscious mind would be revealed. That was exactly true!

Man is like what he believes. If human beings want to change their thoughts and disciplines, they must change their beliefs. This is possible via sending proper signals to the subconscious mind.

MASTERY OF THE DREAM

Is there any relationship between what we see in our dreams and what happens in reality?

- Can our dreams take control of our world?
- Can we take control over our dreams intentionally?
- If it is possible, can we govern wakefulness through dreaming intentionally?

In continuation of their discoveries, ancient masters found out that there is an unspoken relationship between dreams and events in everyday life. Therefore, they proceeded to interpret and analyze dreams and established the knowledge of dream interpretation.

However, as time went on, they asked themselves a question: "Does sleep and its processes affect our wakefulness events?" (In other words, as we dream, something happens in our body that its effects on the universe appear as events that we associate with an interpretation of our dream) Or is this connected universe that creates dreams?

By asking this fundamental question, they stepped in to new era and wondered, if this is true, is it possible to make dream events intentional and take control of wakefulness events?

If we dream that we laugh aloud in a wedding, certainly, in wakefulness, grief and sorrow come toward us and vice versa (note that only part of the dream between spiritual and somatic sleep is interpretable). Now if it was proven that it was the dream that caused events in wakefulness, not occurrences of connected universe, they could create favorite events in their daily life via dreaming intentionally. It means that they could try to cry intentionally in a dream in order to force happiness to trace them!

This experience is easy but also has its own difficulties as well. Staying conscious in a deep sleep was so hard and needed great patience over a long period. However, they were men of action and did not allow the hardships to stop them. Thus, via the invention of diversified methods, they succeeded in this work. Surprisingly, they perceived that what they were thinking was true. How did they do this? They found out that there is a mutual relationship between dreams and wakefulness. It implies that events that occur during dreams can influence daily events and vice versa.

The subconscious mind is part of our being that we cannot dominate consciously. However, it forms our totality. As mentioned before, deep inside of each human being, there is an ocean of power, intelligence, wisdom, capability, and knowledge. Human beings live in an endless ocean of treasures, and they are able to take advantage of unlimited gifts and mental potencies within themselves, and via a wonderful and magical inner power, they can attain happiness, inward calmness, freshness, good health, and wealth, and stay away from bad things such as jealousy, indecencies, depression, and generally all mental and physical sicknesses.

What makes color, sound, solidity, dimension, and space within us? Where have the definitions—based on which our brain builds up color, dimension, and solidity—been recorded? Our seemingly wakeful world is nothing but a picked interpretation of the connected universe that our brain constructs via received surrounding signals, and it only draws us virtual images and feelings that are just a sign of the truth. No world exists outside us with such specifications.

Where is the origin of these interpretations, explanations, and codings that the mind puts over waves? In other words, if we build our wakeful world within ourselves (regarding what we said about channels in previous chapter), are we able to rebuild it as we want? Can we take the control of the dream realm as we became more able to build our wakeful world? Can the subconscious mind, dominate surroundings at high levels via telepathy ability? Can it prepare a means to dominate creatures via suggesting a person's thoughts and demands to the environment and others?

You may have heard from predecessors that using bad language causes evil. Is it possible that our thoughts as well as our dispatched mental activity waves to our surroundings influence our environmental occurrences, people's behaviors toward us, and also our diversified social and personal situations?

During dreaming, human beings' thoughts and perceptions involve nonrelated and unnecessary problems, far less than during a state of wakefulness. Thus, power and potency of the subconscious mind and dispatched telepathy waves via the brain, like laser rays, become many times as much as during wakefulness. Thus, the resulting effects become more obvious and greater than during wakefulness. This influence is divided into some main categories:

1. Influence on the totality of oneself
2. Influence on acquaintances and strangers
3. Influence on the universe
4. Influence on one's totality

To understand better, it is necessary to take a brief look at hypnotism that is artificial sleep. Dr. James Braid first used *hypnotism* or *hypnosis*, which is a derived expression from Greek word *hypnoses*, which means "sleep." The ancientness of the hypnotism phenomenon is too long and turns back to a thousand years BC. Hypnotism is a phenomenon that, in spite of the extraordinary progress of human knowledge and the passing of the twentieth century, has kept its mystical aspect, especially among ordinary people. Hypnosis is a sleepy state in which one's subconscious mind becomes accessible for the hypnotizer.

Hypnotism is a set of suggestions and autosuggestions. Suggestion is a mental induction which produces a special mental condition in the subject. In fact, hypnotism is the state of intensive mental concentration; it implies, contrary to a normal state, in which our mind has diversified and scattered thoughts, in a state of hypnosis concentration, that the mind is empty of irritating thoughts and is unaware of anything except what we suggest.

In such conditions, the subject may not feel the most powerful pain. When a person goes into a deep hypnotic sleep in association with depth of sleep, up to 90 percent of body functions can be affected remarkably via hypnotizer suggestions. This includes skin blistering and burning without fire, no feeling of pain, local numbness, nausea, and loss of memory. Hypnotism also may cause color-blindness, omission of smell or taste sense, particular frequencies being inaudible, happiness or sadness, changes in the five senses, improving intelligence and memory, producing strong telepathies, adjustment or agitation of endocrine glands' performance and hormones, strengthening the immunity system, and healing some incurable sicknesses, as well as cause diversified sicknesses.

Hypnotism has a close relationship with the nervous system so hypnotizer can put the subject into a deep sleep with power of suggestion and will. During hypnotism, different parts of the brain with diversified thoughts will stop and concentrate on a unique subject. In this state, suggestion is started, and one accepts suggested thoughts. The more suggestible the person is, the faster and better the person becomes hypnotized.

In hypnotism, in terms of a highly suggestible subject and deep sleep, an addiction or a passion can be deleted or created. We can also delete or replace internal definitions of life and ideology by hypnotism.

Self-hypnotism is a state in which both subject and hypnotizer are the same. It means the person puts himself in a condition of hypnotic sleep. Ancient masters looked for this territory. However, attaining this skill is so hard to the extent that person must practice so hard for many years to practice self-hypnotism.

Some people make a mistake by considering relaxation and autosuggestion as deep self-hypnotism. Nevertheless, I must notify that self-hypnotism is a very hard and specialized matter. In self-hypnotism, a person can change even his palate and can dream what he wants in a way that his observations become so real that events can be perceived via five senses. For instance, if he assumes himself in a garden, he must see it obviously, hear the voices clearly, and perceive environmental tastes and smells. In such a case, a person can see not only his favorite occurrences, but can also imagine himself in any form he wills so that his subconscious mind along with his mental power implements his demands. The subconscious via affecting our brain and nervous system take control of our body.

It is true that under hypnosis, human beings can influence his mental and physical mood. Thus, by achieving a deep self-hypnotism, we are able to make any changes and alterations to our both body and mind—changes that may appear as miracles. However, the truth is that the human being himself is the miracle of creation.

Those who are familiar with the brain and nervous system put a high value on word *suggestion*. They state that words and suggestions influence endocrine glands and cause a person to get well or become sick. Fear, sorrow, worry, and many other negative feelings (that are nothing but some sort of internal definitions we have about ourselves, surroundings, relatives, etc.) enter the brain via real or imaginary suggestion and put stress on the epiphysis ; the epiphysis secretes an excessive matter called STH. This matter enters other endocrine glands and body organs via the blood and causes diversified illnesses. In contrast, positive feelings such as love, hope, tenderness, happiness, and calmness causes the epiphysis to secrete a matter called ICH, which neutralizes STH, and consequently, the person heals, or it prevents intensification of pain to say the least.

In one experiment, scientists measured the power of an athlete on a power gauge device and one hundred pounds resulted. Whenever an athlete applied greater pressure, the number did not go beyond one hundred pounds. In hypnotism, they suggested to him that he is a powerful man and they measured his power again and then the hand of the device showed 125 lb. In fact, what caused power to increase was the alteration of one belief, one thought, and one definition deep inside his subconscious mind, which was only possible in hypnotism; therefore, replacement of one thought in the subconscious mind can affect the structure and functions of our body deeply.

Thus, ancient masters found out that, via taking control of a dream, they can not only use its benefits for bodily relaxation but they can also dominate the totality of the body, and consequently, they can pave the way for an appearance of the subconscious mind power and their real abilities. Hence, some of these masters preferred to teach their disciples in hypnotism, charisma, heightened awareness, and trance states because in this condition, memory, power of perception, and mental process increase and the mind becomes more powerful in understanding complicated concepts; since, in a short time, by keeping away from logical barriers, they could attain greater practical results.

In fact, they perceived that a human being, more than being a physical body, is a thought, a belief, and a library of definitions and true-false conventions. Our body is a three-dimensional view of these thoughts.

Now it is good to know that no one knows this kind of self-hypnotism now, but he trains and uses relaxation, concentration, and some kind of meditation. You must be careful with untrue claims of deceitful people in this field.

Influence on Acquaintances and Strangers

This kind of influence is accomplished via two ways: firstly, occupation of a part of mind and subsequently telepathy. Secondly, suggestibility that leads to unnoticeable hypnotism. When you become acquainted with someone, it may lead to friendship or enmity. Especially in deep friendships and familiarities, your definition of personality, appearance, name, sign, and the other social-behavioral parameters—also your expectation from him and his expectation from you as well as your definitions about him—will be engraved in your mind.

Hereafter, you save and fix these definitions repeatedly in a hidden corner of yourself via internal dialogue and memory review. This causes establishment of telepathic communication between you through your thoughts, mental moods, beliefs, actions, emotions, and feelings due to somehow concentrating on him (and vice versa), especially in the case that their relationship has found its way to deeper levels of subconscious mind.

According to an explanation of telepathy, the telepathic communication establishes between two creatures when there is a sensorial or recognizable relationship between sender and accepter, no matter whether friendship or enmity, the deeper the relationship is, the higher the intensity of this connection would be. The relationship between plant and human being is evidence for this. Here, the importance of selecting a proper friend can be recognized better since friendship with unrighteous and capricious ones (people that are not healthy from mental and social point of view) causes sick thoughts and feelings in the form of temptation, internal dialogues, unhealthy intentions, sorrow, grief, etc.

In hypnotism, changes happen in bodily physiology. The heart rhythm changes, blood pressure decreases, and peripheral blood vessels resistance reduces as well as the basic metabolisms reduce. Moreover, body temperature, skin electrical resistance, and number and depth of breathing decrease. Hypnotic suggestions make changes in muscle tone and endocrine gland secretion. These changes are basics of some interesting hypnotic phenomena as well as phenomena that can cause remedial influences. Some hypnotic phenomena are as follows: catalepsy or muscle stiffness, hypnotic numbness, making changes in memory power, recalling past ages, extraordinary suggestibility, etc.

In fact, all instances of hypnotism are self-hypnotic, and self-hypnotism is nothing but intentional control of a dream. In hypnotism, someone else guides the subject in order to settle in a trance condition with his own skills, then suggests necessary things to subject. In self-hypnotism, the person himself acts as a guide and controls the remedial process himself. In self-hypnotism, the importance of imagination is much more than concentration, which is used in ordinary hypnotism.

In most of remedial methods of hypnotherapy, self-hypnotism is part of the remedial program. This method is used as a treatment for creating self-reliance, increasing healing expectancy, speeding up the process of wellness, panic control, gaining calmness, making a patient compatible with sickness, increasing the quality of patients' life, pain reduction, etc. Also, in order to increase memory power and learning, increase power of concentration and social skills, as well as succeed in different aspects of life, it is beneficial widely among people specially students.

In hypnotism, because of mental calmness and concentration of the mind on a unique subject, the brain is able to establish the telepathic connection with more intensity and transfers its thoughts and feelings to relatives, friends, or enemies as well, as it becomes aware of their thoughts and feelings.

Ancient masters, via knowing the facts along with their skills, attained via self-hypnotism the ability to see anyone they wanted in their intentional dream, imagine him in the form of a dream, and with the aid of five senses, they were transferring their own thoughts and feelings to that person. This caused formation of strong feelings in the accepter, and subsequently, he surrendered to the sender's demands unintentionally. Of course, at the beginning, it was attractive, but gradually, they understood that the effort for domination over their fellow men was foolish and absurd, and no upright human would allow himself to do so.

Especially when they noticed that this activity caused the seekers to get involved in a bigger trap, it not only prevented eternal salvation and growth but also caused the truth seeker to be ruined. The desire for domination over humankind and forcing them to do the masters' personal demands originates from a need or desire, and each desire is the sign of lack of control on the part of our being which has captivated us unintentionally—captivity that does not present any consequence but devastation of awareness and fragmentation of perception.

They had a higher goal. They wanted to make the totality of awareness and perception intentional, so they concentrated on the unique goal, like a laser ray. So they focused their art of the intentional dream (self-hypnotism) on the most pure and perfect thing that human being knew—God—in a way that even space-time could not restrict. Thus, not only would they be able to discover the absolute realities but they could also release themselves from the space-time restriction. They especially noticed that paying attention to others due to transferred waves and telepathic connections between them resulted in being influenced by internal circumstances and the real nature of others. It was a mean to add the other perception filter, so it inevitably influences the inner world built by the mind.

Human beings, according to their internal descriptions about themselves and others, assume themselves very seriously, importantly, and highly. These feelings are so important to them to the extent that they allow themselves to expect others to support their feelings; whenever things are in contrast to their tendencies, they feel annoyed and offended and start feeling pity for themselves, as well as assume their behavior as a sign of the powerful, important, and right personality.

Now each familiarity, depending on its type, would go along with one new mental tie regarding the relationship type, conditions, and feelings of the opponent person; it can be positive or negative.

Self-importance is one of the biggest mental and psychological problems of human beings. One cannot truly see his surrounding world and break free from perceptional filters while one believes that he is the most important creature of universe. Perceptional filters are collections of mankind's descriptions and memories, which human beings record and save in their mind during their lifetime— descriptions such as colors, smells, tastes, shapes, beliefs, ceremonies, behaviors, good and bad, ugliness and beauty, knowledge, people, etc. These filters will never be omitted. They show their influence during decision making, judgments, occurrences, and events in the form of diversified feelings.

If someone has been kidnapped and beaten in childhood by people in blue dresses, after sixty years, as soon as he sees a blue dress, he would become fearful and hate the blue dress, even if that memory has been deleted from his mind.

Each of these perceptional memories devotes a distinguished part of our attention to themselves. This means fragmentation of perception; subsequently, this makes some part of perception, which perceives surrounding stimuli, misty and unrecognizable. Thus, the highest rate of attention and mental power is squandered by self-conceit and selfishness. We waste away most of our mental energy to show our importance.

For instance, we are always worried extensively about our appearance, so we continuously ask ourselves whether others, especially those who know us, acknowledge us or not. Do they like us? Are we important to them? Have they believed the masks we put on our real face? To what extent have they been deceived by our words and dress? Have we gained superiority over them? Have they accepted us?

These questions are so deep and important for us to the extent that, unintentionally, we bear in mind all manners of our fellow men; to gain access and in order to get the answers, we make an effort to analyze people's behaviors via our perceptional memory and from internal definition and our point of view. The results of these analyses are clear! The sicker we are, the more wrongful our interpretations about our fellow men's behaviors would be. This is the beginning of irritation, sorrow, grief, expectations, friendships, and enmities. It is interesting to know that sometimes our fellow men's behaviors become important to us to the extent that, during our lifetime and all through the daytime, we are engaged in analyzing them, so we consume our total mental energy for this purpose. Moreover, with all these sick thoughts, we expect ourselves to reach gnostics' level!

For instance, you may meet people who in spite of many years passing after one special event get busy retelling that event and analyzing all aspects of it. When you pay attention to the nature of the event, you will find it absurd. For example, one may say, "Why, at that party, did he talk to me that way? Why did he offer the food to her first?"

Think about it—what makes us weak, annoyed, hopeless, happy, unhappy, or hopeful are the feelings of annoyance and offensiveness regarding the deeds and misdeeds of others. In Castaneda's book,[7] Don Juan mentions that "self-importance is our greatest enemy. Our

---

[7]   *The Fire from Within*

self-importance requires that we spend most of our lives offended by someone. Without self-importance we are invulnerable."

Ancient masters found out that deletion of this great mental occupation makes human beings capable of perceiving themselves and the existing world more clearly. They also discovered, via hypnotism, the possibility of omitting most of these dialogues or memories is more feasible. Therefore, psychologists utilize hypnotism to delete many abnormal memories.

They discovered that if someone takes control of his dream, he cannot only have a deeper influence on his fellow men, but he can also stay away from their influences.

Human beings are naturally suggestive in a way that we can say, "All human beings subsist in a hypnotic sleep during their life span in which their hypnotizers are their relatives and their internal dialogues." From early childhood, we have been exposed to many suggestions of our relatives in the form of behaviors, sayings, smells, tastes, colors, feelings, shapes, etc. As time passes, these suggestions build our viewpoints and ideological basics due to life and the surrounding world.

Pay more attention! What you observe as human beings, beings, and occurrences are not the reality! It is what you perceive through your personal eyeglasses. It means

What you see is nearly part of your being . . .

You see the eyeglasses you wear . . .

You are the observers of your perceptional forms.

You see and judge people based on what you are within yourself . . .

Even your outlook about the existing world and God is mostly from your internal definitions.

Your expectations and demands, your acceptance and nonacceptance . . .

Your beliefs, good and evil, ugliness and beauty . . .

Your overall appearance, behavior, conversation and movements . . .

All and all are nothing but yourself as well as definitions you saved within yourself during your lifetime. Thus, as long as you are full of wrong, absurd, nonlogical definitions, you cannot perceive the world as it is truly. Therefore, you will be always wrong.

Our world is a formation of colors, smells, sounds, tastes, etc., that forms the foundation of our feelings, thoughts and beliefs, while all of them are our mental dreams that do not exist outside of us in this form. In fact, the hypnotizers of the connected universe govern our dreams skillfully.

One of the great masters says, "Human beings are the observers, unaware of the fact that their perceived world is nothing but an illusion. An illusion that has been constructed via a description that has been portrayed for them from early childhood. Hence, actually, the world that their rationality wants to hold is the world with fanatic and unquestionable rules; their world has been created since their logic has learned to accept and support it."

Human beings are constantly surrounded by suggestions, instincts, rumors, and advertisements. Therefore, each sound production and chatting, image or occurrence, or any other excitation that is being experienced, causes special suggestive influence on human beings, especially when we continuously concentrate our attention on others' words and actions—others who are our direct hypnotizers as we talk about them in our mind.

Have you ever noticed that when you are sitting in a gathering, they talk about the world, money, income, trading, house buying, sexual desires, pleasures, and recreation, and you are unintentionally attracted to this world? You easily forget religious ways, and if you leave that meeting and go to a spiritual gathering, after a short time passes, you will hate this world and its attractions, so you will be passionate about seeking the truth. This is the sign from that very same hypnotic sleep which we have gone deep into from early childhood, so this rapid influence is the sign of your suggestibility regarding environment.

In fact, we as human beings stabilize and save environmental influences via our internal dialogues and review of what has happened before. If we stop talking about our world and ourselves within ourselves, the world will be what it has to be, since we intensify and renew it and fix it through internal dialogue. We do it on and on until the day we die.

We are slaves to environmental suggestions that our friends and relatives have mostly formed. We look at each occurrence and event through the prism of our senses and perceptional filters. This means that we see the environment and people in a way that has been suggested to us.

Identically, a person sees a stone as an apple and vice versa in hypnotism. We see human beings not the way they really are, but we see them in a way that our perceptional filters and forms permit. We, as human beings, have gone into a deep sleep. This is because we do not understand anything as it is due to ourselves, the universe, our friends and enemies, and creatures' and others' beliefs. Therefore, a miserable selfishness surrounds us in a way that we do not assume anyone being entitled except ourselves. What we perceive from the environment and human beings is mostly an interpretation; we relate to them based on our internal descriptions, beliefs, experiences, knowledge, and perceptional memories.

Our friends and relatives, moment by moment, cause us to become stable in this hypnotic sleep via suggestion of their beliefs. Moreover, the interesting thing is that we keep ourselves in this trap through internal dialogue in their absence. Hence, it is clear that our personality, feelings, thoughts, and mental and even physical health surprisingly depend on our relatives, family, and close friends.

Ancient masters discovered that it is possible to wake up from this hypnotic dream and see the world and its creatures as they are. This is possible through taking control of dreams and not paying attention to whatever has been created in us via suggestions such as our anger, worry, annoyance, jealousy, etc. This requires staying calm, harnessing inner turbulences, not judging others, not expecting others along with not hurting yourself due to others, quieting down internal dialogue, not reviewing unnecessary things continuously, not becoming offended by others, etc.

Communities, in which people take part, and friends they choose are of great importance. The one who wants to be free from this dream through understanding that the effects of suggestions are unavoidable and that they influence him, whether he wants or not, will be scrupulous enough to take part in such gatherings or to choose friends.

Captivating human beings in perceptional molds causes one to establish one code in his subconscious mind as soon as he meets someone. In this way, the subconscious mind can provide a telepathic connection between you and others via contacting the other human's subconscious mind (telepathy). Many spiritual dreams and awareness of future events are achieved via the subconscious mind's connection and deductions during dreaming.

In one experience, the hypnotizer asked a footballer to put his hand on the table. Then, it was suggested to him that his hand was stuck to the table. In spite of his efforts, he could not lift his hand. In another experience, they suggested a weight lifting champion that he was incapable of lifting a pencil. The weight lifter was not able to lift a pencil, whereas under normal conditions, he could elevate a two-hundred-kilogram weight. Such influences in body functions show the effect of suggestions in a human's mental and physical health. Therefore, via taking control of the dream, we will be able to influence others, our surroundings, and ourselves.

Negative thoughts affect our body and mind, the same as what happens in hypnosis. The effect of suggestion on human beings is so powerful that it can make him sick or release him from acute diseases.

Children of each nation, from early childhood, go down deep into a belief in sleep via suggestions of their adults. In addition, they are trained to fear to think about their ancestors' beliefs or ask questions about their trained beliefs. They mostly do not dare to think about their questions, so they escape from any argument and discussion that questions their beliefs. This kind of training transfers from one generation to the next one; however, in many cases, whenever such people face to logical questions compulsorily and are not able to answer, as they are setting afoot some mottos, begin to fight with questions as they consider them the best answer.

Advertisements and rumors are established because people are constantly in a hypnotic sleep; thus, they work due to humans' suggestible nature. The more precisely these advertisements and rumors are designed, the greater their effects are, especially when they are repeated many times, and people, intentionally or unintentionally, will be influenced by them.

INFLUENCE IN CONNECTING
WITH THE UNIVERSE

If a person's intent can influence the rate of inner calmness or turbulence of a plant, is it not able to appear in forms of diversified physical and mental moods in other beings? Does it affect the growth or actions of beings around?

As explained before, we see that human beings can influence the environment as he is influenced by the environment too. The Quran says, "Thus, decay and corruption appears in sea and land because of people actions." A good person with pleasing thoughts, as facing others, can influence their behavioral reactions spontaneously due to the calmness that he inspires in them. Contrarily, people who have abnormal thoughts have negative influences.

Observing these connections, we can understand that the possibility of deeper and wider influence on the connected universe in intentional sleep (very deep self-hypnotism) is more than wakefulness. Therefore, if someone in an intentional dream perceives that he is merciful to a plant or a flower, it would grow more than if it were in its natural state.

Thus, we can find the great rule of the universe: The universe, like one part of a human's body, is influenced by him and feels him. If a human being extinguishes his inner turbulences, he can touch the universe, communicate with it, and make changes in it. Furthermore, a human being in both wakefulness and sleep is hypnotized. There are differences between the two. In wakefulness, he has greater conscious control over his actions in comparison to sleep conditions, but the world of dreams has a greater influence on the body and the universe. Real freedom is secured by waking up from both dreams, which is achieved via releasing ourselves from paying attention to our environment and our relatives' suggestions. Whenever we stop analyzing and judging relatives and the existing universe as well as extinguishing our internal dialogue and quieting down our mind's turbulences due to paying attention to others, inner conventions, and our desires, it is time that we can see the existing universe and ourselves truly and reach real freedom and true wakefulness.

The world is spawned by our wakefulness dream, and we have devoted our totality due to this hellish dream to the extent that we are ready to die for it.

THE OPPOSITES

The belief of domination of two powers—good and bad, light and darkness, yen and yang, Ahura Mazda and Ahriman, positive and negative, attraction and repulsion, etc.—over the universe is so fundamental that it has not only influenced physics but also penetrated all philosophies and schools. In all religions and schools, you can trace its footprints. Many philosophers and thinkers believe that everything finds its meaning via its opposites, such as matter and antimatter, darkness and light, heat and coolness, positive and negative charge.

Believing in the existence of opposites in many religions has even proceeded to the extent that they have assumed two gods for the existing universe—gods that are constantly fighting with each other. However, do opposites really exist?

Matter and elements, due to imperfectness of the five senses, appear in our inner world along with opposites. Such as light and darkness that are two sides of one coin, we perceive lack of light as darkness. Under normal conditions, human beings are only able to see three spectrums out of the uncountable spectrums of light, and wherever these three spectrums do not exist, we call it a dark place. Thus, we are only able to see things that can reflect these three spectrums.

Darkness does not exist, and murkiness is the extinction of our senses and does not exist beyond our mind.

O thou who seeks reality! Be aware that the world goes on only and only within you . . . and outside . . .

Were the thinkers and philosophers who claimed they were looking for were the truth not aware of this fact?

Did they not know that opposites were just our minds' creations within us and the real world was free from any opposites?

If our eyes could observe all magnetic waves, would darkness, shadow, and murkiness have any meaning?

During sunset when darkness spreads its shadow over the universe's stage, you could describe this event as follows: "My inner darkness and night arrived, and part of my senses' imperfectness appeared." In fact, opposites are spawned by your perceptional channels' imperfectness, and what you call opposite is nothing but the manifestation of the imperfection of your cage.

We perceive the world imperfectly, so we consider it separated and full of opposites, but no opposites exist in the real world.

O thou seekers of reality and searchers of mysteries, it is necessary to be aware that the continuation of the world depends on your imperfectness, and it remains stable until you are imperfect. When you start becoming perfect, your world collapses and then the present world would not exist anymore!

See, if before knowing ourselves, we make an effort to work on words such as *God, world, human being,* and *resurrection,* we will certainly come to know anything except their real meaning. This is our inner world that has created a world of opposites, not the external world. In the real world, opposites lose their meanings.

Heat and coolness, darkness and luminance, sour and sweet, soft and rough, silence and noise, ugly and beautiful, good and bad, right and wrong, pain and pleasure, etc., are the words that imperfection of our perception channels has conveyed meaning to. They have turned our inner world into a battlefield—a battle that has formed our happiness, sorrow, pleasure, and pain.

Look at your life, beliefs, thoughts, deliberations and feelings, pains and pleasures, then pay attention to sentences and principles of diversified schools. See how your observed world and its opposites form them?

To what extent have you taken the world you see seriously?

If you pay more attention, you will find that not only are all your intellectual and persuasive fundamentals based on taking your inner dream as reality, but also in all self-contemplations, judgments, and theologies, you have always tried to describe and justify realities based on your inner world.

Meanwhile, human descriptions of life, world, total self, and others have been appeared as perceptional filters. In addition, people, via attributing descriptions to opposites of their inner world, add new filtering layers to their own world in a way that they make that imperfect inner world—which is the result of their senses' imperfectness—more imperfect. Thus, the more imperfect our perceptional channels—and subsequently, our internal filters—are, the more hellish our world would be. Moreover, if the opposites and filters reduce, our world would be closer to happiness, beauty, and kindness.

Our definitions of good and bad, ugliness and beauty, prohibited and permissible, right and wrong, recommended and indispensable, social and conventional form our perceptional filters. We are busy reviewing these perceptional filters to the extent that no opportunity and no mental energy is left for perceiving and discovering realities.

We perceive a limited spectrum of energy that our senses are sensitive to, and we are incapable of perceiving other states, just like antimatter that is not perceivable via material senses. The more the deficient our perception channels are, the greater the opposites of our inner world would be, so it would build up a hellish life for us.

As mentioned in the previous chapter, human beings, during their worldly life, live in a deep hypnotic sleep. Being impressed by relative suggestions in different forms of education, knowledge, beliefs, customs, etc., people assume their inner world very seriously, and by definitions that they learn through the lapse of time, they divide their inner world into important and unimportant parts. They spend their mental and psychological power for their beliefs. At a party, one woman may pay more attention to others' appearance and movements rather than their reality since they have been defined as important to her.

We learn to make descriptions about ourselves, relatives, things and materials, occurrences and future events in ourselves firstly, then we base our expectations, due to our environment and others, on these wrong definitions. Then we accuse anyone who does not obey these rules of stepping on certain rights of ours and arrange punishments for them. Finally, we mobilize the totality of ourselves for imposing these definitions on others and ourselves.

Thus, the amount of happiness and sorrow we acquire depends on the degree of failures and successes that we attain in this despotic battle.

Now we completely forget that the truth of things, the people and the world's beings, is completely different from what we perceive, and our descriptions and definitions cannot be applied to them. Our quarrel for placing the real world in our mental forms (molds) and mental definitions completely seems like an attempt of a little ant to stop the planet earth from rotating.

Each human being has a so-called description about his personality, which consists of social position, overall appearance, understanding and intelligence, ability, perception, justice, kindness, loyalty, and other attributes of his inner side. It makes him define his expectations of his environment, relatives, and their rights based on this so-called personality (perceptional mask), and consequently, it builds up a weighing criterion for behaviors in his conscious mind. In the case of not being satisfied, he becomes depressed and finds himself oppressed. Therefore, he begins to pity himself and goes on to the extent that animosity, anger, revenge, and jealousy fill him up, and destroys himself or the other person.

Depression, peptic ulcer, nervous system weakness, battles, animosities and annoyances, chronic headaches, many heart attacks, and cerebral apoplexy, etc., all originate from these definitions.

The older one gets, the more he fixes these rules and definitions via his internal dialogues, so he practically provides a hell for himself and others.

If, in this endless battle, personal failures prevail over his successes, he begins to pity himself over how oppressed he is. Actually, the totality of his mental energy is being devoted to the extent that he is not able to perceive environmental stimuli, even on a macroscopic scale.

If you feed a wolf and it attacks you and bites you, you will not be affected by depression or animosity, and you will not review its actions for months in your mind. This is since, based on definitions you have in your mind about a wolf, you do not count it as a disgraceful thing and assume it is something natural. Thus, you have no inner struggle about it. If it were a human, you would encounter diversified inner struggles since it is not predicted based on your descriptions about a human; and this originates from our stupidity and wrong rearing wherein we do not accept everyone with his own nature. Instead, we want to convince him to be placed within our inner descriptions.

We have learned to deceive ourselves instead of accepting the world, so we always live in an undetermined future or nonexisting past. This is the main reason for not perceiving the world's realities.

From early childhood, we teach our children unintentionally to grieve and take people's words seriously as well as self-importance, selfishness, attracting others, and so many other unbecoming attributes. They become the calamity of their life. Hence, we send a person to society whose mind is completely busy due to analyzing people's behaviors. In addition, in order to gain access to his main goals, he expenses the totality of himself. In this state, how can you expect such a person to perceive the truth of the existing universe?

He is born. He drowns himself in the game of destiny, plays with his mental images, and dreams, especially those images he thinks are of his fellow men. He grieves, deceives himself via internal dialogues, then becomes old, disabled, and finally dies without having time to think about the reason of his coming and going. It is at the time of death that he understands who he was and where he came from. He understands the reality of the world. However, it would be too late to know.

Hearing Channel

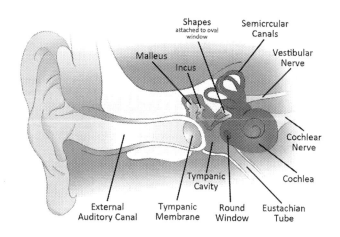

Ears are the channels of the hearing sense that work with waves and vibrations in the air. These channels are able to perceive waves with frequencies between 20 and 20,000 hertz or wavelengths between 17 m to 2 cm. Like the optic channel, the hearing channel causes neurotic excitation and nerve pulsation. However, in the optic channel, light causes this excitation, whereas in the ear, mechanical movement causes it. It is the difference between a microphone and a photocell; both of them produce electricity, but one of them produces it mechanically and the other one via light.

Most invertebrate animals live in a silent world. Among this group, just a few arthropods—including lobsters, spiders, and insects—have a hearing device. Among insects, only locusts, crickets, and many butterflies have an ear.

In vertebrate animals, there is also the true organ of the hearing sense, which is called the organ of Corti, embedded in cochlea. Fishes do not have a middle and external ear; their hearing system only includes an inner ear. Amphibians, creepers, and birds also have a middle ear; but they do not have an auricle. In mammalians, the external ear has been developed, which plays an important role in determining the direction of sound.

Physiology of Ears

In human beings, the ear consists of three basic parts: the outer ear, the middle ear, and the inner ear.

The Outer Ear

This part includes the auricle and auditory canal. The auricle distinguishes sound direction, and the auditory canal conducts sound waves to the middle ear. The tympanic membrane (eardrum) is placed at the end of the auditory canal. This eardrum, at the time of contacting sound waves, is vibrating. In the auditory canal, a sticky, brown, and bitter matter covers the opening of the canal, avoiding the entrance of insects and dust into the canal.

The Middle Ear

The middle ear consists of a bony cavity in which there are three ossicles: malleus, incus, and stapes. These ossicles connect the eardrum to the oval window. The oval window is placed between the middle ear and the cochlea. These ossicles not only transfer sound vibrations to the cochlea but also adjust their intensity.

A canal which has been extended from the middle ear to the pharynx is called a stash horn. The air enters the middle ear (at the back of eardrum) via this canal. If this is not done, the eardrum will not vibrate perfectly.

The Inner Ear (Cochlea)

The inner ear consists of a bony and membranous labyrinth. This membranous labyrinth includes fluid bags that are placed in a cavity of the temporal bone (the bony labyrinth). The bony labyrinth consists of the vestibule, half-circular canal, and cochlea parts. A part of the membranous labyrinth known as cochlear canal is located in cochlea. The cochlea is twisted around a spongy, bony axis called the modiolus two and half times. The labyrinth section is formed by two sacs, the utricle and the saccule. There are three half-circle canals. They are perpendicular relative to each other. There are ciliate cells in the sacs and canals mentioned before.

The cilia of these cells are in a jelly liquid, which is firm to some extent. Whenever we move our head, the jelly liquid moves; it stimulates ciliate cells, and consequently, they create nervous messages. The nervous messages go to the cerebellum via a special nerve, so it causes us to become aware of our imbalance. The cochlea is twisted like a conch. The hearing receptors are in this section.

In our ears, sounds make the liquid tremble in cochlea. This vibration can just vibrate specific chords as the result of a phenomenon known as voice intensification. The more the frequencies there are, the more the shorter cords vibrate. Since the length of these cords cannot be shorter than a minimum limit, we are not able to hear voices with frequencies that are greater than a specific limit.

The cochlea part is a one-centimeter closed twisted box that contains a liquid. One side of this box is narrower, and it culminates in the inner ear. The box analyzes different sounds like a filter and selects frequencies between twenty and twenty thousand hertz. Then it sends them into the inner part. Different frequencies reach a maximum level in different sections of this box. The higher frequencies are measured in the section that is closer to the nozzle of the box, while the lower ones are evaluated in the upper section. There are also nervous cells that are stimulated before the vibrations of the liquid in the box.

The interesting point in recent research is that the frequencies are analyzed in a simple and ordinary box. The researchers had thought the only reason for contortion of the cochlea box is to make better use of space. According to this concept, they had an artificial ear designed in the form of straight pipes without contortion. Later, Manusaki and his cooperators found that whenever sound waves pass through the cochlea part, their energies are not distributed monotonously in different parts of the box, but they gather along the outer septum of the box. In this manner, a large quantity of energy is centralized in the upper part, in the opposite side of the entrance nozzle. We can see this phenomenon in some places like the court of the Isfahan historical Mosque in Isfahan or Saint Paul's Cathedral in London. We can hear the humming of people who are in a corner of the court clearly far from them. Gathering of energy in one part of the cochlear box helps the membranous cells reveal sound waves better.

In this manner, the sensitivity degree of the upper part of the cochlear box is higher, and the lower frequencies can be received better. Therefore, the cochlea is like an amplifier to relay the lower frequencies.

THE TRUTH OF THE VOICE

Sound is nothing but the fluctuation of air molecules around us. The level of loudness of one voice (low-pitched or high-pitched) is one of the properties of sound waves, which is frequency. Frequency is the number of vibrations per second and is measured in hertz. A high-pitched sound corresponds to a high-frequency sound wave and a low-pitched sound corresponds to a low-frequency sound wave. The higher the frequency is, the more high-pitched the voice would be and vice versa. The power and intensity of one sound depends on the power of sound waves that are measured in decibel (db) units. With each ten-decibel increase in power, the heard voice would be two times greater. Therefore, a voice with ninety-decibel intensity would be two times more powerful than a voice at eighty decibels. Normally, a conversation between two people is done in the range of sixty decibels. The intensity of busy street traffic sounds is almost eighty decibels. Staying in an environment where noise is over 120 decibels, even for a short time, can harm our hearing. Our ability to decompose compound voices such as music and determine the rate of voice loudness, which can be heard by human beings, differs from one person to another. The ability to hear high-frequency voices decreases by age. Some animals such as bats and dogs can detect sounds with frequencies higher than a human being's normal range.

Ultrasound waves and sound waves are of the same nature, and the way they are produced and emitted are the same. However, the ultrasound waves do not affect a human being's auditory system. Different animals detect different ranges of sound waves. For instance, a dog detects frequencies as high as forty thousand hertz, whereas frequencies as high as eighty thousand hertz affect a bat's sense of hearing. Some insects can hear frequencies up to 175,000 hertz, and they can also produce these waves to communicate with each other.

In human beings, sounds with a low frequency are detected in the frontal and external part, and sounds with a high frequency are detected in the back and inner part of the hearing system. In fact, this is the sound height that is being coded in the auditory cortex of the brain, not the frequency. Individual neurons in the auditory cortex respond to parameters such as starting point, continuation, duration, and repetition of frequency of a sonic stimulus, especially in the direction that the wave sound extends. The auditory cortex deals with sonic patterns, sound property analysis, and determination of dwelling place. Damage in the superior temporal auditory communicative cortex causes disorders in short-term memory.

A human being determines the sound direction via two main mechanisms:
1. Discrepancy between the times of sound entrance into each ear
2. Discrepancy between the intensity of sound in each ear

The first mechanism works for frequencies lower than three thousand hertz, and the second one works for higher frequencies. Whenever one settles directly in front of the sound source, sound reaches both ears at the same time, while if the right ear is closer to the sound source, the dispatched signals from right ear will enter the brain faster than dispatched signals from the left ear.

The auditory lobe of brain, which processes received data from ears, is the place for saving musical melodies in human beings. The researchers of Dartmouth University, via doing experiments, observed that each time people listen to a song that is familiar to them, in the case of deleting some fragments of the song randomly, the auditory part of brain automatically extracts the omitted part and adds it to the existing part. Their investigation confirms other research that had been done on sensory data associated with visual information. Those experiments also revealed that part of the brain cortex that processes visual data, during watching a familiar image in which some parts of picture had been deleted, completes the deleted parts by using memory information.

These experiments prove that in a human being's brain, some parts that are in charge of data processing simultaneously record these kinds of information as well. The researchers in these experiments noticed that the human brain acts differently in rebuilding omitted parts of a song, and this method depends mostly on the kind of music. For instance, when instrumental music is being broadcast, the back part of the brain is activated for rebuilding musical parts, while if it is broadcast along with words, the frontal part of brain is in charge of restructuring it.

The received messages from the optic and hearing channels via neurons are of the same nature. What makes the difference between these two perceptions is the place in which these messages are being processed. Sound, light, and color, all and all, are metaphorical realities that do not exist out of our perception in this way that we feel. Beings' perception puts sensorial label on signals due to the channels via which they have been received.

It means that if one wave is received from the hearing channel, it will be perceived as sound, and if it is being perceived via the optic channel, it will be in the form of color and luminance. If it could be possible to perceive visual messages via the hearing channel and auditory messages via the optic channel, then air movements and vibrations would have been perceived as color and luminance, and electromagnetic waves (light) would be perceived as sound. Thus, one could witness the world in which the sound sources flicker as shining lights and would disappear by turning the ears away. He also would perceive light sources as sounds that are perceived often in the form of continuous whistling and would become silent by closing the eyes. In fact, all waves can be perceived as sound! This is true, provided they stimulate neurons via the hearing channel and they can be perceived in the form of colors and diversified lights provided they excite neurons via the optic channel.

These two properties, color and sound, are not natural characteristics of waves but an interpretation that our perception applies to received nervous impulses through the hearing and optic channels.

If we connect a nervous fiber of the tongue to a nerve that connects an ear to the brain, we would hear the shocking sound of an explosion by leaking a vinegar drop onto the tongue. Actually, an illusion happens in this way. A drug or mental pressure creates short circuits among some sensory parts of brain so that music is received in brain in the form of light patterns. Therefore, what we assume as a sensible quality completely depends on the part that is being excited in the brain.

Nervous fibers are long and tiny cells that, as soon as they are excited, not only produce electrical charges but also transfer these charges via a set of chemical changes, which slip like a ring along it with a speed of 320 km per hour. This phenomenon always stays steady. Both the current and the speed of transfer are always constant, and nothing happens unless the phenomenon ends. If a more powerful signal is received from the environment, it cannot produce a greater electrical charge. Thus, the sensation intensity, in a way that brain distinguishes, only depends on electrical pulses.

Many examples exist in nature of species that perceive sound as light. The Mexican blind cave fish is of this type. This fish, by propagating sound waves and receiving its reflections via a channel similar to our hearing channel, draws an image of the world since its eyes are completely blind. A kind of beetle causes continuous patterns of circular waves on the water's surface, and via received reflections of these waves, draws a black-and-white world. The farther the barrier is, the darker the image would be and vice versa. Therefore, such creatures are even able to distinguish a fine hole on a coral body.

If we were to perceive sound stimuli as it is, we would perceive only vibrational movement—like the time your hand is placed on a vibrating plate—not in a way we feel now in which no vibration exists.

Sound is a kind of perceptional sensation and dream, which is indescribable, and since we have been used to it since childhood, we cannot imagine that voice does not exist in the world with such quality. This feeling only relates to our inner world. The outer world is soundless.

Of course, for attaining calmness, nature prepares silence via restricting the hearing channel to definite wavelengths as well as transforming air movement into a kind of perception that we call sound or silence. It produces feeling, which makes us distinguish the difference and intensity of waves. Sound is a beautiful and indescribable feeling that we are not able to describe even for ourselves—a feeling spawned by movement.

- The world is silent.
- The world is soundless and quiet.
- The world is continuously in a roaring turbulence.
- There is no song, no whisper, no raving, and no noise.
- All of these are turmoils of your inner world.
- See to what extent what happens inside you—and you call it the world—is different from what happens in reality.
- How do you want to know God?
- Upon what reality have you constructed the basis of being or not being, the trueness or falseness, of your beliefs?

What a beautiful saying our holy Prophet Mohammed has: "If the one knows himself, he will know his God."

Say "ooooo" with a loud and extended voice and listen to it. Now try to explain for yourself how you perceive the vibrated movement of the air! I mean, describe what you perceive (hear) as you imagine the main event. Consider, when you say "ooooo," that the air vibration would be as in image A, and when you say "Tee tee tee tee tee," it would be in the form of pattern B.

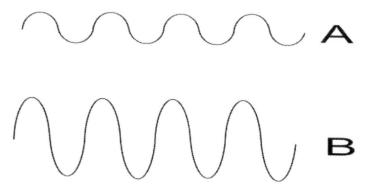

Now ask yourself why we hear the "ooooo" sound when the air particles fluctuate in the form of A, and it is heard as "Tee tee tee tee tee" when they conform to pattern B. Why does it not happen conversely? On what basis does our brain put sonic labels on these stimuli? The more important thing—can we say that the brain of human beings and other creatures, regarding the fact that sound is a perceptional label and has been built by our mind, build a unique stimulus in the same form of sound?

Are you sure what you hear as "ooooo" cannot be heard by someone else as "Tee tee tee tee tee"? You may say it is not possible since we all utter it with a unique voice and write it differently as well. However, when you are asked to explain what you have heard, in reply, you produce similar waves with your vocal cords instead of answering. You just say, "I heard this—'ooooo.'" In other words, this answer takes us to that same initial point: how do you know I perceive this wave as you hear it?

Suppose when wave AB (previous image) comes to the observer Z, he feels it as sound OT. When that exact wave reaches observer X, he hears it as sound NA, and both observers choose this compounded voice as a name for water. When the observer Z asks X how he hears the voice (that same wave AB), observer X, who perceives the mentioned wave with the sound NA, produces a wave similar to

AB, and observer Z receives it as OT. Subsequently, Z thinks that observer X also hears wave AB as he has heard it.

In fact, we are unable to describe what we hear, but we put a unique name on a unique wave and relate it to one subject. In a way that we remember that thing anytime we hear that sound, that is how our inner worlds are hidden behind words and agreements; all of us agree upon this hallucination that the world of all beings is the same.

A nightingale sings.

Another nightingale listens to it from a far distance.

A cat that is ambushed among bushes listens to it either.

Below a sunshade, a family consisting of a father, a mother, and a child sit and enjoy this sweet song. However, none of them hear a unique voice.

If it were possible to travel through each other's inner world, then we would face diversified voices—voices that are related to another bird and none of those heard voices are the nightingales' sounds.

Inside each being, the sound of a nightingale, cloud, thunder, music, noise, etc., is a unique sound—a sound which no one can hear.

The auditory limits and sound labels that the brain associates with the sounds are not acquirable or elective, but they are inborn qualities. It implies that the human being himself is not involved in it. We are not able to define to hear wave A as "ooooo" or wave B as "Tee tee tee tee tee," but mental stimuli and nervous messages have been defined before, in the part of our being in which the act of interpretation and transformation of environmental messages to sensory data are done.

According to these descriptions, our brain transforms nervous signals into sensory messages. In fact, this is our creator that has taught us how to receive stimuli.

Beings hear environmental waves in a form that has been defined within them, then relate new concepts and agreements to those sounds and communicate to each other on that basis. Factually, do not think that everybody hears the voice of another being or the sound of a piano as you hear.

The connected universe has created a distinguished voice with a unique frequency for each being—the voice through which they express their inner events to the others, so they communicate universally. However, this voice assignment has not only been done by chance, but no other creature can also hear it as the being itself hears it.

The Quran's hint about *bayan* reveals that the limits, quality, frequency, and condition of voices that human beings can produce are not intentional, but the creator of the universe has taught them before to do so. However, human beings used this common language for creating agreements and new codes between themselves, and finally, people invented languages.

Perception has an immaterial nature, and different parts of brain factually work as an antenna that after interpretation and coding of a wave, it is dispatched to perception. We will explain it later in the following volumes. Now it must be noted that mentioned topics regarding perceptions do not lead us to nullity, but it implies that our perception of stimuli is different from the stimuli itself. However, many of these stimuli have a reality outside of our metaphorical world.

Now look at your beliefs once more. How seriously have you taken this dream?

We might say that Adam was not exiled from heaven, but due to eating the forbidden fruit (hallucination tree), he went down into a deep sleep and was beset by illusion—an illusion that he named the world.

TASTE AND SMELL CHANNELS

These two channels are chemical receptors that, in connection with materials, recognize the poolside collections and create taste and smell regarding their effects on their frameworks. In fact, palpable information of taste and smell cells help us to respond to our nourishing needs and help us avoid harmful materials.

TASTE PHYSIOLOGY

Chemical receptors, including palpable cells available in the nose and taste sprouts, are sensitive to chemical materials around them. In these receptors, one receptor cell, in response to a chemical material solution in the liquid (e.g., salvia or the liquid covering the inner surface of the mouth), produces reception potential.

One of the most sensitive chemical receptors can be found in male silkworm moth's feelers. Thousands of fine hairs cover these feelers. The fine hairs are chemical receptors that identify the sexually attractive material known as bombykol, produced by female silkworm moth. When each fine hair (around fifty per second) identifies one bombykol cell, the male silkworm moth begins to reply to the female one. The taste cells are located in taste sprouts, which are mainly on the surface of the tongue and soft palate of the mouth. The main taste sprouts are located on the surface of the tongue and in papillae. The papillae are short villouslike processors that make our tongue velvety-shaped. However, a great number of papillae named threadlike papillae lack taste sprouts, and they are effective in sensing touch.

The most important papillae are fungiform papillae that have taste sprouts and are in the front of the tongue. These fungiform papillae are pink points around the sides of the tongue. They can be seen after drinking milk. At the back of the tongue, there are twelve bigger taste sprouts known as wall-type papillae that are in the form of the number 8. Taste sprouts are onion-shaped structures with fifty to one hundred taste cells. Each of them has a fingerlike process known as microvilli, which are rooted from the pore just right over taste sprouts, called the taste cavity. Chemical materials are melted in salvia and attached to the taste cells via the taste cavity. There, these materials react with proteins on the surface of the cells that are known as taste receptors. This reaction can be accomplished with proteins known as ion channels. It finally leads to electrical signal alteration, which makes them ready to produce chemical signals for the excitation of neurons.

The taste cells, like nervous ones, have some negative charges inside and some positive charges outside. The materials, reacting with proteins cells, change ionic charge distribution conditions and cause an increase in positive ions inside the cells. This depolarization causes the taste cells to release chemical materials known as neurotransmitters. The chemical material stimulates nervous cells that are associated with taste cells and dispatches electrical messages to the brain.

In spite of our beliefs, the taste receptors are not only sensitive to four tastes (bitterness, acidity, sweetness, saltiness); but also, their sensibility to the tastes can be varied according to reaction between materials and the taste cells. Sometimes the combination of several tastes can induce a new taste in the perception of beings.

The acidic taste is produced because of acid, which means the H^+ ion. The perception intensity of this taste is proportionate to the logarithm of the H^+ ion density. Na, mainly, creates the salty taste that is created via ionized salts. The quality of salinity differs from each other. Some salts stimulate the sense of salinity as well as other taste senses. The positive ions of salt are more responsible than the anions of the salt for salinity. Special chemical materials do not produce the sweetness. Some materials causing the sweetness are as follows: hydrocarbons, glycols, alcohols, aldehydes, ketones, amides, esters, some amino acids, some small proteins, sulfonic acids, halogenic acids, mineral salts of lead, and berylliums. Note that the materials causing the sweetness are organic chemical materials. The bitterness is not just caused by one special chemical material as well. Two main groups of materials that establish the bitterness taste are as follows:

1. Organic materials with long chain containing nitrogen (N)
2. Alkaloids, which are used in most medicines. It includes quinine, caffeine, strychnine, and nicotine.

Many materials firstly cause the sweetness, then establish the bitterness. This is true about saccharine. Many fatal toxins existing in poisonous plants are of alkaloid type.

In low density, each taste sprout usually responds to one stimulant; however, in high density, these taste sprouts can respond to two or more tastes.

The mechanism by which the most stimulant materials react with taste cilia is sticking the taste producer chemical materials to protein molecule receptors that are knobbed out via villous membrane. This causes the ion channels to be opened and allows the Na^+ ions to enter the cells and depolarize them. Then the exciting chemical material is gradually washed away from the taste cilium by salvia, and in this manner, the stimulant factor is omitted. This means the taste cells of earlier beings had known these materials and created protein receptors conformably.

The chemical materials causing salinity and acidity act directly via ionic channels. Sweet and bitter materials are transferred to sublime receptors while causing signals in the cells and finally culminating to open and close channels. The brain perceives these instigations in the form of delight or unpleasant taste due to information received from the constructing elements of our own figures and data due to the effects of materials on our own chemical figure that have them innately. Thus, with the tendency toward pleasure and wanting to escape from torment, beings choose materials as foods that are necessary for their body and do not have bad effects.

Eating perfect foods is just as important as not eating harmful foods. Poisonous mixtures like strychnine, other herbaceous alkaloids, alcoholic drinks, etc., have a violent bitter taste that causes beings to escape from this kind of materials by provoking a sense of torment.

TASTES

The perception of beings in the animal and vegetal realms will be calm and motionless when all of their body constructor elements are adequate and balanced. However, if the minimal deficiencies disturb this equilibrium, the perception and ego would be excited and would react. This response appears as torment and pleasure in the form of carnal desires, such as inclination for various flavors, hunger and thirst, desiring special food or meals, libido, and inclination for smells and colors. Briefly, it produces various feelings and mental conditions; finally, it incites and carries into effect the living creature to attain perceptional balance and calmness.

For instance, the animals that have their adrenal glands taken out of their bodies, and so are empty of salt, show more tendency toward salty water.

Furthermore, the animals that suffer from sugar scarcity due to insulin injection automatically select the sweet meals among various edibles. The animals which encountered a parathyroidectomy and lack calcium spontaneously select water with high calcium chloride content.

In this state, beings, by showing special mental and corporeal actions, feel some kind of restlessness and unusual sense and finally reveal it in various forms such as impatience, excitement, irritability, depression, feebleness, etc. In such situations, due to excitation, the creatures may encounter changes in their tastes and tendencies—tastes and tendencies such as flavors, smells, shapes, and colors (in the next chapters, you will find out that the cosmos, via influencing our life, contributes to these taste alterations, but these changes are universal and epidemic). Therefore, they turn to special actions and movements in order to overcome these states and to reach calmness, so that they can gain the preceding balance via compensation of that deficiency or excreting excesses.

Hence, the human being's tendencies and tastes are changing. Tendencies and tastes can be used as predictive factors to prevent physical and mental problems. Colors psychology, face detection, and similar sciences originate from these internal and mental changes arising from perceptional balance disturbance. In the field of color psychology, this taste alteration causes the subject of an experiment, each in a different mental and psychic state, to choose from a diversified arrangement of color cards which are set in front of him, and the doctor comes to know the psychic state of his patient due to his selection.

Regarding this matter, it can be concluded that correct and natural nutrition and avoiding unnatural and junk food (such as puff, chocolates, cookies, or soft drinks) or fried food can affect a human's mental and psychological health and may even cure an illness. Herbivory and hydrotherapy are some methods of treatment via healthy nourishment.

Sometimes people, being excited by covering materials (the materials/drugs that reduce the pain instead of remedy the problem), may perceive spurious calmness and balance, and via dreaming that their pain is gone, might even be annihilated. Narcotic substances, cigarettes, alcoholic liquor, imaginative medicines, and even sedatives are of these categories.

In human beings that are sensible and are able to use instruments, this state is considered as confrontation of body and mind. It means that, as body can affect mind, thoughts and feelings can affect shortcomings and tendencies of our body. In other words, as any insufficiency or deficiency causes a diversified mental and psychic state; conversely, thoughts, ponderings, intentions, and different psychic states can directly influence our body, whether apparently (on our face) or inwardly (on different organs such as stomach, heart, etc.).

Pain and pleasure arising from materials and foods, apart from their tastes, depends on produced conditions in the being's body as well, which is so-called conditioning.

For example, if a person, during eating a sweet meal, becomes irritated, he will unintentionally hate that taste, and he may feel pain. In other words, pain and pleasure concerning tastes does not only depend on the taste itself, but it can be changed under different circumstances, including memories and occurrences. In fact, when our perception receives chemical signals from our tongue and nose in the form of taste and smell, respectively, it can give those signals new meanings in terms of the existing condition (corporeal and/or psychic pain or pleasure, whichever is dominant at that moment). Thus, *it* corrects the previous meaning, like correcting the meaning of a word and applying a new/distinct meaning to it.

Smell and taste are not the inherent qualities/properties of materials, but these are labels our perception applies to recognize the chemical configuration schema of materials, so our perception incites pain and pleasure in beings via creating sensations of taste and smell in awareness. In this way, it helps them in the recognition of the body's needs as well as encourages and exhorts them to eat.

In fact, our perception knows how the body works, what is necessary for it, and what harms it. Consequently, it classifies the necessary materials in the pleasure category and harmful ones in the pain category. That is why living creatures often tend to eat or smell, because it creates pleasure arising from collision of elements on the tongue, while it is not due to their nutritive value. *The pain-pleasure rule says that none of the creatures carry into effect, unless for gaining pleasure or eluding torment.*

Look at yourself and others. What is the motive behind their actions?

Who are the determiners, intellect and logic or pleasure and pain?

If you look at people's lives honestly, even people who choose a monastic life, you would realize that 99 percent of their exertions are because they want to gain more pleasure or elude a greater pain. Even a monk or hermit obeys the pain-pleasure rule rather than following his intellect (i.e., in order to gain more pleasure in the hereafter, stay away from vale pleasures, or for escaping from the hereafter's enormous torments, tolerate all vale suffering).

Taste is the figurative sensation that does not exist outside of mind and perception, and so like other world parameters/characteristics, only confines itself inside of beings, and due to different necessities of creatures to survive, their perceptions of tastes and smells vary. For instance, the excrement of some animals has a singular and appetizing taste and smell for some insects, while it is stinky and unsavory for human beings. That is because insects do not perceive its taste and smell as human beings do, even if transmittal nervous pulses from the tongue to brain are the same for both creatures.

Similarity, the transmitted nervous pulses from sensory channels to the brain do not lead to equal perception. It is the same as used language among human beings, although similar nervous pulses are transmitted from a unique sound, but no similar perception occurs. In fact, people perceive signals corresponding to their appropriate definitions/descriptions of the sound or nervous pulses.

For instance, English and Persian listeners hear the word *cheese* identically, but their perceptions are completely different. Undoubtedly, there are some exceptions; to give an example, some materials are harmful and injurious despite their pleasant taste and smell. The reason must be investigated for substance limitation and imperfectness of physical body as well as its composition. It may be because sometimes a harmful material is mixed with a necessary material and conceals itself behind its taste and smell; as it enters body, it harms the organic systems.

Due to differences in creature's necessities and their bodies' physical/chemical structure, their taste and smell perceptions, concerns about a unique element can differ completely, whereas there is no sign of any difference. It is since none of them can express his feelings via words; feelings are not measurable. Indeed, nobody can say what the color which he names red is or how he/she perceives a sour taste, although similar nervous pulses are transmitted to the brain from the stimulus.

While talking, more than referring to our real feelings of stimuli such as smell, taste, color, or sound, we point to the stimulus itself. The names we put on these stimuli are rather agreements by which we remind each other's preceding memories about that special taste or smell. In fact, when you ask someone, "How this fruit taste?" He says in response, "It tastes the same as you taste."

As we explained before, materials and elements do not have an intrinsic difference, but their differences only arise from shape, multiplicity, and the arrangement of their forming particles. The taste and smell channels transmit the differences as nervous pulses to brain, and perception perceives them as the senses of taste and smell.

SMELL

The smelling sense can be understood as weakened tasting sense because this channel is highly sensitive on a molecular scale to suspended materials in the air. Whenever these molecules and separated parts of elements collide with smell villi, they incite nervous cells by producing a series of chemical reactions and consequently transmit a message proportionate to incitation intensity and material type to the brain. This message is accessible for awareness via the brain and is being perceived as the smell sense.

Taste, smell, color, sound and silence, brightness and darkness, thoroughly, just restrict to internal and perceptual world of beings in the form of figurative realities.

Each being has its own special and unique world and imagines that all other creatures perceive the world as it does (although their worlds have an identical skeleton). These perceptional differences outside of beings' minds lead to the appearance of diversified tendencies, dispositions, senses, and mentalities that are the main reason for most of conflicts, oppositions, enmities, and battles. In humankind, especially, they cause the establishment of different religions, rules of life, insights, tendencies, and deviations of religion, as well as branching out of religion.

Consider four particles—proton, neutron, electron, and positron—that are located at a distinguished distance from each other in a way that they can be influenced by repulsive and gravitational force.

Now we poll from three particles—proton, neutron, and electron—concerning positron, which has positive charge. The electron with a negative charge will say, "Positron is such an attractive, nice, affable, and conversable particle." While the proton will submit its protest to the electron and will say, "Positron is a nonsociable, bad-tempered, and secluded particle; it repels everyone and makes all other particles suffer." The neutron, who is still silent, will submit its protest in a pitiable manner to both other particles and will say, "Why do you go to extremes in your judgment and do not observe temperance? Positron is not what the proton and the electron state, but it is a calm and silent particle and does not bother anyone; it does not repel or attract anyone."

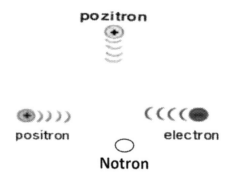

Which one tells the truth?

Which of them is right?

If you were in the judgment position, what would your vote be?

If the particles do not accept your opinion and continue arguing, what will they conclude?

Even if their discussions are logical, when will they come to a conclusion?

More importantly, what would be their opinion regarding themselves and other particles?

These three viewpoints about the positron are all true and false in this court of law. In fact, the positron is not any of presented definitions. However, the above particles do not take lies as well.

The positron, inherently, has no properties/characteristics, and the aforementioned particles elucidate their perceptions, which appear in the form of three completely different senses in their own inner world. They want to justify the reality with their figurative world that dominates their perceptions. Since their inner world is not similar to each other, the perceptual differences appear in the form of different opinions, tendencies, inconsistencies, etc., and cause misunderstandings among them. Thus, he imagines that others observe thinks as he does. Therefore, whenever someone talks or behaves contrary to another one's statement, he will be exposed to criticism, reproach, and partially quarrel.

TACTILE CHANNEL

The tactile channel is a door that makes us familiar with feelings such as heat and cold, softness and roughness, solidity and hardness of things, space surfaces (size), and helps us in rebuilding our inner world, or let's say it deceives us!

Physiology of the Tactile Channel

Our skin has pain receptors, temperature receptors (for heat and cold), and mechanical receptors (for touching and pressure). Each of these receptors are dendrites composed of one or multiple neurons, which are transformers of stimulus influence. They finally send the resulted action potencies to the central nervous system. In other words, each neuron in a skin receptor is used simultaneously as a receiving cell and sensory neuron.

Pain is an important sense since it is often the sign of danger and usually forces an animal to repair themselves. Pain can also inform us of injury or illness. All parts of body except the brain have pain receivers.

Thermoreceptors in skin reveal heat or coolness. Other thermoreceptors that are placed deep inside the body show blood temperature. The hypothalamus is the main thermostat of body, which keeps body temperature constant in a limited and determined range while receiving action potencies from superficial and deep thermoreceptors of the body.

Mechanical receptors are various. Diversified kinds of these receptors are excited via different forms of mechanical energies such as touching, pressing, pulling, movement and sound. All these forces use their influences via bending or extension of the plasma membrane of a receptor cell. When a membrane is being deformed, it becomes more penetrable regarding positive ions, and if the stimulus is powerful enough, exciting mechanical energy turns into potential energy of the receptor.

Two kinds of mechanical receptors turn trivial inputs of mechanical energy to action potency. The third type is the pressure receptor, which is placed in a deeper part of skin and is excited via high-pressure stimuli. The fourth kind of mechanical receptor is the touch receptor of hair and organs, which manifests hair movements.

The touch receptor of the feeler base of a cat or a bear is too sensitive, and they are able to distinguish near objects via touching in darkness. There are two other kinds of mechanical receptors—mechanical receptors of blood pressure, which can be found in some blood veins, and sensory receptors of skeleton muscles.

A. Heat and Coolness

Heat and coolness are not opposite or separated words, but are two imaginations, two dreams, and two different feelings about one reality that is being created via the tactile channel. These two feelings make beings conscious of dangers, arising from faster or slower movement of body molecules called temperature via producing pain and pleasure in them, so that those feelings can adjust temperature via different methods.

Thermal variations of creatures' bodies or, in other words, the movement variation of body molecules depends on different factors. These factors are divided into two main parts—wave and matter. Wave factors are illuminated electromagnetic waves that make contact with constructing atoms and molecules of a creature's body directly, and by transferring their energy to these atoms and molecules, cause movement to increase in them. These waves are called thermal waves, provided that their wavelength is around eight hundred nanometers. Waves with wavelengths shorter than four hundred nanometers cause damage due to their high energy, and wavelengths higher than eight hundred nanometers have no tangible effect because of their small energy. Increasing movement and vibration of body molecules creates the feeling of heat.

Electrons are in a normal state, intent to preserve previous energy levels, so when they are motivated by thermal waves, this tendency causes electrons to propagate absorbed waves after a short time and return to their previous equilibrium state.

This absorption-propagation circuit of energy via electrons causes continuous fluctuation in atoms and molecules. If absorbed waves are equal to propagated waves, the fluctuation of molecules will be constant, but if the absorbed waves are more than propagated waves, the fluctuation will increase momentarily. Living beings feel the increase of fluctuation intensity of molecules as rising body temperature. Now if propagated waves are more than absorbed waves, these fluctuations decrease and living creatures will feel coolness. The sun, fire, burning of foodstuff in body cells, etc., are wave production sources.

Now let's talk about material factors—the material factors that change the fluctuation of body-constructing particles—are the friction and collision of particles with each other; they cause transformation of movement and fluctuation to nearby molecules. During this process, living creatures, instead of perceiving movement in their body, perceive heat and coolness. If they were able to perceive what really happens, they would feel some kind of vibration, which reduces or induces constantly. However, the perception misinterprets this reality beautifully, so we feel this movement as the sense of heat or coolness.

Our tactile channel feels motion and waves as heat and coolness . . .

Our ear feels motion and waves as sound . . .

Our eyes feel waves as color and illumination . . .

What is common among the senses is motion, motion, and motion . . .

In fact, our inner world is spawned via different interpretations of our senses due to movements and fluctuations of the endless ocean of energy which surrounds us. We are floating over it like bubbles—the bubbles which have produced a charming dream within them, so we have engaged ourselves in it. The roaring waves of this endless ocean direct and control our dreams via five outlets of our bubbles.

The body of all beings consists of particles called atoms and molecules. These atoms are always busy fluctuating. This implies that our body is vibrating continuously. Whenever the rate of this fluctuation increases, we experience a feeling called heat; and whenever it reduces, the sense of coolness arises.

If the rate of body particle fluctuation exceeds, the rate of collision between atoms and molecules increases, and this causes harmful chemical variations, including decomposition or composition of harmful effects. Thus, beings feel it as heat, fever, or burns and consequently feel tortured and then resort to everything in order to stay away from heat as they seek temperature reduction agents.

The movements and fluctuations of body molecules between minimum and maximum limits cause immunization of molecular tissues as well as cause vital intercellular reactions. Thus, beings feel less-more rather than this minimal-maximal limit as pain; also, they feel fluctuations between these two boundaries as pleasure with diversified intensity. Therefore, they are continuously struggling to earn pleasure and escape from pain in order to retain their body temperature between these two boundaries.

In fact, heat and coolness are two figurative and illusory feelings of one reality, and there is no similarity between those feelings and the reality.

Such feelings just cause pain and pleasure in beings, which is the only motive of beings. It seems that these senses and channels are not arranged to understand the truth as they are. They put creatures into practice via creating pain and pleasure (the unique and only understandable language for beings) unintentionally and lead them to survive. They create animal life, which is also called carnal (material) life.

Pain and pleasure are considered as a penalty-prize system by which the connected universe carries beings into effect compulsorily and gives meaning to their vital activities. In addition, it encourages or discourages them for obeying or disobeying its rules.

A man and a woman—due to their instinctive attractiveness, not to have a child—are attracted to each other. They marry and compulsorily have a child. In fact, they resign themselves to do so due to instinctual force, so that a baby can step into the world. Since the connected universe demands this action by force, in return, it offers them sexual pleasure, love of a child, and love of a spouse. After birth, taking pleasure from the child's beauty and innocence is the reward the connected universe gives them, and for disobeying these rules, pain appears as a kind of punishment based on their deeds.

The torture that an unrighteous child imposes on his parents is the result of rebellion against existing rules of the universe. It happens via false education or not following important rules of the pregnancy period. Thus, even spiritual reward and punishment is intertwined by deeds themselves in this world; no one can escape from consequences of his deeds. Thus, if anyone acts benevolently, he will see its reward, and if he does something wrong, he will be punished.[8]

The existing universe never demands anything without reward; if nature needs a cleaner for wiping out an animal's corpse, it engages vultures and gives them the pleasure of eating a corpse as a reward, so they will be rewarded to the extent of their efforts. Therefore, their deeds will go along with complete satisfaction, so we can see divine justice as well.

The reward of instinctive deeds can be likened to physical exercises; if you do it incorrectly and wrongfully, it would go along with too many harmful effects. If you exercise on principle, you would see its positive effects. The reward or punishment of physical exercise is hidden behind the activity itself, and it is not imposed on human beings from outside. Any overdoing sporting activities does not end in perfectness, but it causes serious injuries to the body, which is the punishment of going to extremes.

In animal life only the pain and pleasure resulting from body channels' perception, dominate over beings' actions.

They are always seeking for activities that are associated with gaining more pleasure without any necessity to thinking and

---

[8] Quran 99:7-8

searching for reason and truth of those actions and received messages of sense channels, or seeking a reason for their being and their unintentional deeds. Thus, because they become accustomed to logic of bodily pain and pleasure, from the early days of entering material world, they assume it as an undeniable truth, so they reject anything that is not sensible via sensory channels and assume that other beings perceive the world as they do.

There is another story for the human being. Since he owns power of creativity and intelligence and ability to use tools, whenever his intellectual power (intention)—which is a superior awareness regarding matter and ego—weakens and the human gets used to it, this sensuality will destroy him via taking control of his intelligence.

Thought and intelligence are not devoted to intellect, but it is a device in a human's hand that intellect or ego can utilize. When ego takes control of intellect, it is called a trick, deceit, temptation, and inner evil. In this condition, a person becomes more similar to human-faced animal which takes advantage of his intelligence to gain more sensual pleasure regardless of the consequences arising from going to extremes. This part of feelings, which is called sensuous dialogue, originates from the ego. It has nothing to do with truth of motives, the world, and the aim of creation, death, and perfection.

Sometimes, intentionally or unintentionally, our family and relatives train us in a way that says our dream is absolutely true. Then, they put a predefined image and plan of one life in front of us, so we must only seek pleasures based on the plan. We play, go to work, study, marry, have a child, watch movie, laugh, cry, and then die! In all these actions, our reason and logic is gaining more pleasure and calmness. They train us via words or via their acts not to think! Not to ask ourselves such questions as the following: Where are you from? Why have you come? Where will you go? Why will you go? Why must you eat? Why must you sleep? Why must you marry? What is laughter? What is grief? What is color? What is smell? Why do we like some smells and hate others? What is taste? What is the universe? In addition, there are thousands of questions that we never find an opportunity to think about.

Our parents and relatives have taught us that if these sorts of thoughts enter our mind unintentionally, we must consider some as poetic thoughts. They have also taught us indirectly that this kind of knowledge has no practical value. They are only and only for talking, nothing else, and we are not supposed to do what we know! Instead, we must learn how to justify, mislead, and deceive others and ourselves; we have been taught to make up ourselves in order to exhibit a false personality. They have also taught us how to protect this untrue personality through internal dialogue and sacrifice all our mental power for it.

When we hear a subject or achieve a reality, due to our trainings, we pretend the truth is fascinating on the surface, but factually, our enthusiasm is not due to know the truth. We are happy because we have found a new way to deceive others and to make up a new untrue personality. Each person seeks and studies reality on purpose, not for finding an answer, but for escaping from their conscience's torment arising from knowing realities. It is to say a Christian searches for topics in order to prove his beliefs; a Zoroastrian, a Buddhist, a Muslim, and an irreligious one do the same. It is good to know that truthless disciples of these schools only follow those parts of their religion which justifies their personal deeds and actions! While if someone is truly seeking to discover the truth, whether in religious matters or social, personal, or family matters, he will observe problems unbiased and does not fear losing his previous beliefs. It is possible when the person is a real investigator.

Sometimes one says I have heard it is right due to a reliable source. Sometimes he relates stories about unidentified persons, and sometimes he adds one memory of himself to it while none of them are demonstrable. Sometimes people say an event has occurred on that date or it has been written in that holy book! We are used to observing everything from special point of view. If the heard subject goes according to our desire, we accept it without any investigation, and if it does not, we reject it explicitly. This is not the way a real investigator does work.

When a human being performs and acts as an animal and assumes his inner dream as reality along with utilizing his intelligence to justify his actions and his world, actually, he takes his inner dream seriously to the extent that he sacrifices his totality for it. Moreover, his description of life would be wallowing in this dream to gain an animal's pleasure more. Therefore, he basks in the animal life and never reaches his real place. It is the world where color, solidity, things, size, smells and tastes, sounds, and beings—even its events—are all inner dreams that have been built up by human beings' perception. Human beings crucify and torture themselves brutally just in their dreams.

In nature, because of balance among opposites and forming of beings based on connected universe rules, animals cannot go beyond extremes, and since their intelligence is not enough to make changes in nature, the pleasure-seeking and pain-escaping will not end up with their annihilation. There is a precise and firm relationship between creature needs and nature. In other words, beings have been created based on nature's facilities, and intact nature is a perfect surrounding for them. In humankind, who has higher intelligence, it is something else. Due to his knowledge imperfections, its subsequent effects, and results due to making changes in nature, the human being goes to extremes terribly, in such a way that he not only destroys himself but also ruins nature and other beings.

Some of the greatest cases of human destruction through his hands are drug addiction, alcoholism, cruelty, perversion, immorality, and misuse of natural resources—and his motives are to attain excessive pleasure.

SOLIDITY

When you walk on the earth, make contact with a barrier, or perceive solidity and penetrability of matter with your tactile channel, you presume that the wall or the earth is full of matter in a way that particles are placed adjacent to each other intensively and they are full of matter identical to their volumes. What we really observe, proven by the tactile sense, is an untrue volume.

No matter can touch another matter or come into contact with it, except on an atomic scale, like a collision between proton and neutron particles in nuclear explosions, which leads the matter to demolition along with releasing horrible energy.

All materials and elements consist of small particles, so-called atoms. These atoms, in turn, are formed by smaller particles called protons, neutrons, and electrons. In fact, atom is the name of a collection of these three particles. Protons and neutrons are in the atom's center and electrons, with the mass of almost two-thousandth of a proton's mass, spins around the atom nucleus. It seems like a balloon, which embeds a small mass in an extreme volume.

The distance between the atom nucleus and the first orbit of electron, relative to volume of these particles, is in the manner that if we magnify the diameter of an atom nucleus to the extent of a hazelnut, the distance between the electron and atom nucleus would be a half-kilometer. This is the spinning speed close to light speed that exhibits an unreal volume for perception. Consider a luminous rotating object; when it rotates at a high speed, it seems as a big ring of fire instead of an illuminated point. This illusion arises from perceptional channel imperfection.

The fast spinning of electrons around the nucleus, light reflection from electron clouds, and the very slow speed of neuronal message transition from retina to perceptional area, regarding electron spinning speed, cause atoms and molecules to be seen bulky; thus, all elements and matter appear as a collection of adjacent solid balls.

If it could be possible to compress all materials on planet earth in a way that all voids between particles are omitted, the planet by turning into a black hole would have been as big as a basketball. It shows that matter with specified volume has fluctuated in such a big space and has created a virtual image of planet earth.

Contrary to our imagination, things and materials are not bulky, solid. Rather, trivial parts of matter have fluctuated in a huge space, and these fluctuations reflect some visible wavelengths of light.

The propulsive force, arising from nuclear charges of atoms and their electron bubble, causes atoms not to come closer than the allowable extent. If they pass this boundary, they produce chemical compositions by joining electron at their last orbit. Therefore, when materials and elements apparently come into contact with each other, actually, they slip over each other over a microscopic distance. This is like two magnets with homonymous poles which slip over each other due to propulsion between two poles and do not touch each other. Now electromagnetic waves of electron charges act as intermediary whenever materials approach each other and avoid collision.

When you walk on the earth, in fact, you slip on the pillow of electromagnetic waves with a trivial distance from earth in the air and feel the propulsive pressure as solidity. Our tactile sense, just via contacting these waves, produces feelings of hardness, roughness, solidity, etc., which are confirmed by the optic channel. Therefore, these two sensory channels fix this perceptual illusion in beings as an undeniable truth.

When you move your hand toward a wall, the electromagnetic pillow is placed between your hand and the wall, which is the result of electrical charges of material particles. This pillow of waves avoids truly touching the wall by your hand. If you were able to come closer—more than the determined distance—there would be a chemical bound between your hand and the wall. Practically, your hand would be stuck to the wall. Under such conditions, real taction would not occur, since no particle of your body would come into contact with any matter of the wall. This chemical composition establishes itself due to the joining of electrons, not because of taction. Only in one case can the wall be touched—when the constructing particles of your body and the wall exceed the propulsive boundary and reach each other, in this case, a nuclear explosion would happen.

If one day, electrons—these charming painters of existence—stop fluctuating, all things would vanish, and our world would collapse.

However, the most important performance of the tactile channel is not sensing heat and coolness, but the establishment of space, size, and movement. Our inner world forms within us. This means that the initial condition for manifestation of this universe is appearance of space or continuum. The space is the expansion that creates our inside, and the universe comes to view in it. Then movement, time, and space find their meanings. In fact, the tactile sense is one of the essential foundations of our world to survive.

Without the tactile sense, we would not have expansion—subsequently, space, locality, movement, as well as time would lose their meanings.

Tactility is not skin or sensory nerves, but it is a part of our perception which seeks help from skin and nerves to create dreams in our inner world. Our mistake as human beings is that we assume skin and nerves as our tactile sense, while these tools are only under the control of tactility. Insensibility, parallelism, transaction of the spinal cord—all and all—are deficiencies relative to these tools and are not associated with the tactile sense.

Your inner world (dream of senses) spawns via your birth and ends as you die. It has no past and no future.

As explained thoroughly in the "Dimension" discussion, perception of depth and volume (especially your body volume), the ability to consider things separately, being aware of body boundaries—all and all—originate from the tactile sense, and without this sense, none of them are meaningful.

Observe your body; for instance, consider your hands. You are able to feel them and distinguish their beginning and end. You can feel their movement in space.

More than being substance and material, human beings and other living creatures are perception, which has been visible in the world via particles of matter, like a light ray, which a dust particle has made visible.

Material particles are, in fact, fields of energy that float in a space where it is full of waves, and nothing happens in this environment, but it is under the influence of the ocean of waves. This ocean is truly the extension of us and vice versa. This is the illusion of tactility that makes us presume ourselves as a part of this ocean.

Active energy, which is the origin of these two states (matter, wave), can appear in other forms, which is unperceivable to human beings' sense channels, and it can build up worlds with diversified living beings.

Solids, liquids, colors, diversified elements, softness, roughness, gases, smells, tastes, heat and coolness, darkness and illumination, and generally all opposites form an unreal world which is bounded to the inside of beings and does not exist out of their mind in a way they are perceived now. In fact, a human being, during his lifetime, lives in his mind, and all things and substances of his inner world originate from imperfectness of perceptual channels and application of filtration via these channels that are steadily being stabilized through internal dialogue.

Color, light, darkness, shadows, solidity, and all else are a mental imagination of an external truth.

What is the truth?

What has been laid out of our inner world and which has been covered by our being?

Heat and coolness, tastes and smells, softness and roughness, toughness and hardness, solidity of things, and all shapes of our observed world are illusions of our senses.

Dimensions, space, time, movement, and depth are the dreams of our tactile and optic channels.

What really goes on in this world?

Who are we? What are we doing here?

Why do we dream? Why do we have illusion? Why are we far away from reality?

Battles, wars, contradictions, different religions! Opposite beliefs! Which of them are true? Who is the righteous?

Why is it that anytime someone puts up metaphysics for discussion, people escape from thinking about it and resign themselves to blind acceptance?

Of what are we afraid? From what do we escape?

In the world, of which its hunter is death, does fear have any meaning?

In the world, which is nothing but perceptional illusion and imagination, do jealousy, expectation, desire, anger and animosity, cruelty, self-centeredness, pride, and generally all these self-torment and other torment have any meaning? Does it have any value?

Observe the moments of your life; you spend it moment by moment. What is your purpose? For whom do you spend it?

You are in heaven. You are free. You are perfect, only if you know your value. Set yourself free from suggestions of hypnotizers who try to keep you in this deep sleep by incitation of your anger, libido, hopelessness, fear, jealousy, regret, etc., with a strong will.

We have come to this world; in other words, you stepped into this hypnotic sleep to seek perfection. We are not able to be free or to grow without a rival or challenger.

Life and all its contents are factually stealers of our concentration and energy, while if we become able to control our insides, they cause our energy to go up and subsequently make us perfect.

FINAL WORD

- For many years, I observed nonexistence through my prism of senses and thought that I saw existence.
- Then I sacrificed myself for it.
- When I crept out of this prism, I found out that I had sacrificed my existence for nonexistence.
- Thus, I took light of the heart in hand and began to observe; then time became meaningless in me, the depth of sea passed in my eyes, and the secret of the storm flowed in my word.
- Then I looked through existence; I saw nothing but nonexistence.
- I sought nonexistence in order to see existence through it.
- When I reached nonexistence, I saw the being of divine presence. I found out that you can find existence only when you do not exist, and you can find God wherever you cannot find yourself.

www.venakey.com
mohammadbabaee@venakey.com
omb@venakey.com

Books to be published:

1) Consiousness and matter
2) Venakey aura sight
3) Venakey Energy healing
4) Venakey Telepathy
5) (Venakey) A way to health
6) Religous Bandits

www.venakey.com
mohammadbabaee@venakey.com
omb@venakey.com